This book belongs to:

_____

Capricorn Daily Horoscope 2023

Copyright © 2022 by Crystal Sky
Mystic Cat

All rights reserved. This book or any portion thereof may not be copied or used in any manner without the publisher's express written permission except for the use of brief quotations in a book review.

The information accessible from this book is for informational purposes only. No statement within is a promise of benefits. There is no guarantee of any results.

Images are under license from Shutterstock, Dreamstime, Canva, or Depositphotos.

Capricorn
Daily Horoscope 2023

2023

JANUARY
M	T	W	T	F	S	S
						1
2	3	4	5	6	7	8
9	10	11	12	13	14	15
16	17	18	19	20	21	22
23	24	25	26	27	28	29
30	31					

FEBRUARY
M	T	W	T	F	S	S
		1	2	3	4	5
6	7	8	9	10	11	12
13	14	15	16	17	18	19
20	21	22	23	24	25	26
27	28					

MARCH
M	T	W	T	F	S	S
		1	2	3	4	5
6	7	8	9	10	11	12
13	14	15	16	17	18	19
20	21	22	23	24	25	26
27	28	29	30	31		

APRIL
M	T	W	T	F	S	S
					1	2
3	4	5	6	7	8	9
10	11	12	13	14	15	16
17	18	19	20	21	22	23
24	25	26	27	28	29	30

MAY
M	T	W	T	F	S	S
1	2	3	4	5	6	7
8	9	10	11	12	13	14
15	16	17	18	19	20	21
22	23	24	25	26	27	28
29	30	31				

JUNE
M	T	W	T	F	S	S
			1	2	3	4
5	6	7	8	9	10	11
12	13	14	15	16	17	18
19	20	21	22	23	24	25
26	27	28	29	30		

JULY
M	T	W	T	F	S	S
					1	2
3	4	5	6	7	8	9
10	11	12	13	14	15	16
17	18	19	20	21	22	23
24	25	26	27	28	29	30
31						

AUGUST
M	T	W	T	F	S	S
1	2	3	4	5	6	
7	8	9	10	11	12	13
14	15	16	17	18	19	20
21	22	23	24	25	26	27
28	29	30	31			

SEPTEMBER
M	T	W	T	F	S	S
				1	2	3
4	5	6	7	8	9	10
11	12	13	14	15	16	17
18	19	20	21	22	23	24
25	26	27	28	29	30	

OCTOBER
M	T	W	T	F	S	S
						1
2	3	4	5	6	7	8
9	10	11	12	13	14	15
16	17	18	19	20	21	22
23	24	25	26	27	28	29
30	31					

NOVEMBER
M	T	W	T	F	S	S
		1	2	3	4	5
6	7	8	9	10	11	12
13	14	15	16	17	18	19
20	21	22	23	24	25	26
27	28	29	30			

DECEMBER
M	T	W	T	F	S	S
				1	2	3
4	5	6	7	8	9	10
11	12	13	14	15	16	17
18	19	20	21	22	23	24
25	26	27	28	29	30	31

2023 AT A GLANCE

Eclipses

Hybrid Solar – April 20th

Penumbral Lunar – May 5th

Annular Solar – October 14th

Partial Lunar -October 28th

Equinoxes and Solstices

Spring - March 20th 21:25

Summer - June 21st 14:52

Fall – September 23rd 06:50

Winter – December 22nd 03:28

Mercury Retrogrades

December 29th, 2022 Capricorn - January 18th Capricorn

April 21st Taurus – May 15th Taurus

August 23rd Virgo – September 15th Virgo

December 13th Capricorn - January 2nd, 2024 Sagittarius

2023 FULL MOONS

Wolf Moon: January 6th, 23:09

Snow Moon: February 5th, 18:30

Worm Moon March 7th, 12:40

Pink Moon: April 6th, 4:37

Flower Moon: May 5th, 17:34

Strawberry Moon: June 4th, 3:42

Buck Moon: July 3rd, 11:40

Sturgeon Moon: August 1st, 18:32

Blue Moon: August 31st, 1:36

Corn, Harvest Moon: September 29th, 9:58

Hunters Moon: October 28th, 20:23

Beaver Moon: November 27th, 9:16

Cold Moon: December 27th, 0:34

2023 INGRESSES

Mars Ingresses

Mar 25, 2023, 11:36	Mars enters Cancer
May 20, 2023, 15:24	Mars enters Leo
Jul 10, 2023, 11:34	Mars enters Virgo
Aug 27, 2023, 13:15	Mars enters Libra
Oct 12, 2023, 3:39	Mars enters Scorpio
Nov 24, 2023, 10:10	Mars enters Sagittarius

Venus Ingresses

Jan 3, 2023, 2:06	Venus enters Aquarius
Jan 27, 2023, 2:29	Venus enters Pisces
Feb 20, 2023, 7:52	Venus enters Aries
Mar 16, 2023, 22:31	Venus enters Taurus
Apr 11, 2023, 4:43	Venus enters Gemini
May 7, 2023, 14:20	Venus enters Cancer
Jun 5, 2023, 13:42	Venus enters Leo
Oct 9, 2023, 1:06	Venus enters Virgo
Nov 8, 2023, 9:27	Venus enters Libra
Dec 4, 2023, 18:48	Venus enters Scorpio
Dec 29, 2023, 20:21	Venus enters Sagittarius

Mercury Ingresses

Feb 11, 2023, 11:22	Mercury enters Aquarius
Mar 2, 2023, 22:49	Mercury enters Pisces
Mar 19, 2023, 04:22	Mercury enters Aries
Apr 3, 2023, 16:20	Mercury enters Taurus
Jun 11, 2023, 10:24	Mercury enters Gemini
Jun 27, 2023, 0:22	Mercury enters Cancer
Jul 11, 2023, 4:09	Mercury enters Leo
Jul 28, 2023, 21:29	Mercury enters Virgo
Oct 5, 2023, 0:06	Mercury enters Libra
Oct 22, 2023, 6:46	Mercury enters Scorpio
Nov 10, 2023, 6:22	Mercury enters Sagittarius
Dec 1, 2023, 14:29	Mercury enters Capricorn

Slower Moving Ingresses

Mar 7, 2023, 13:03	Saturn enters Pisces
Mar 23, 2023, 8:42	Pluto enters Aquarius
May 16, 2023, 17:01	Jupiter enters Taurus

The Moon Phases

- New Moon (Dark Moon)
- Waxing Crescent Moon
- First Quarter Moon
- Waxing Gibbous Moon
- Full Moon
- Waning Gibbous (Disseminating) Moon
- Third (Last/Reconciling) Quarter Moon
- Waning Crescent (Balsamic) Moon

● New Moon (Dark Moon)

The New Moon reveals what hides beyond the realm of everyday circumstances. It creates space to focus on contemplation and the gathering of wisdom. It is the beginning of the moon cycles. It is a time for plotting your course and planning for the future. It does let you unearth new possibilities when you tap into the wisdom of what is flying under the radar. You can embrace positivity, change, and adaptability. Harness the New Moon's power to set the stage for developing your trailblazing ideas. It is a Moon phase for hatching plans for nurturing ideas. Creativity is quickening; thoughts are flexible and innovative. Epiphanies are prevalent during this time.

● Waxing Crescent Moon

It is the Moon's first step forward on her journey towards fullness. Change is in the air, it can feel challenging to see the path ahead, yet something is tempting you forward. Excitement and inspiration are in the air. It epitomizes a willingness to be open to change and grow your world. This Moon often brings surprises, good news, seed money, and secret information. This Moon brings opportunities that are a catalyst for change. It tempts the debut of wild ideas and goals. It catapults you towards growth and often brings a breakthrough that sweeps in and demands your attention. Changes in the air inspiration weave the threads of manifestation around your awareness.

🌓 First Quarter Moon

The First Quarter Moon is when exactly half of the Moon is shining. It signifies that action is ready to be taken. You face a crossroads; decisive action clears the path. You cut through indecisiveness and make your way forward. There is a sense of something growing during this phase. Your creativity nourishes the seeds you planted. As you reflect on this journey, you draw equilibrium and balance the First Quarter Moon's energy before tipping the scales in your favor. You feel a sense of accomplishment of having made progress on your journey, yet, there is still a long way to go. Pause, take time to contemplate the path ahead, and nurture your sense of perseverance and grit, as things have a ways to go.

🌔 Waxing Gibbous Moon

Your plans are growing; the devil is in the detail; a meticulous approach lets you achieve the highest result. You may find a boost arrives and gives a shot of can-do energy. It connects you with new information about the path ahead. The Moon is growing, as is your creativity, inspiration, and focus. It is also a time of essential adjustments, streamlining, evaluating goals, and plotting your course towards the final destination. Success is within reach; a final push will get you through. The wind is beneath your wings, a conclusion within reach, and you have the tools at your disposal to achieve your vision.

Full Moon

The Full Moon is when you often reach a successful conclusion. It does bring a bounty that adds to your harvest. Something unexpected often unfolds that transforms your experience. It catches you by surprise, a breath of fresh air; it is a magical time that lets you appreciate what your work has achieved. It is time for communication and sharing thoughts and ideas. It often brings a revelation eliminating new information. The path clears, and you release doubt, anxiety, and tension. It is a therapeutic and healing time that lets you release old energy positively and supportively.

Waning Gibbous (Disseminating) Moon

The Waning gibbous Moon is perfect for release; it allows you to cut away from areas that hold back true potential. You may feel drained as you have worked hard, journeyed long, and are now creating space to return and complete the cycle. It does see tools arrive to support and nourish your spirit. Creating space to channel your energy effectively and cutting away outworn regions creates an environment that lets your ideas and efforts bloom. It is a healing time, a time of acceptance that things move forward towards completing a cycle. This casting off the outworn debris that accumulates over the lunar month is a vital cleansing that clears space and resolves complex emotions that may cling to your energy if not addressed.

🌗 Third (Last/Reconciling) Quarter Moon

This Moon is about stabilizing your foundations. There is uncertainty shifting sands; as change surrounds your life, take time to be mindful of drawing balance into your world. It is the perfect time to reconnect with simple past times and hobbies. Securing and tethering your energy does build a stable foundation from which to grow your world. It is time to take stock and balance areas of your life. Consolidating your power by nurturing your inner child lets you embrace a chapter to focus on the areas that bring you joy. It is not time to advance or acquire new goals. The restful phase speaks of simple pastimes that nurture your spirit.

🌘 Waning Crescent (Balsamic) Moon

The Waning Crescent Moon completes the cycle; this Moon finishes the set. It lets you tie up loose ends, finish the finer details, and create space for new inspiration to flow into your world once the cycle begins. The word balsamic speaks of healing and attending to areas that feel raw or sensitive. It is a mystical phase that reconnects you to the process of life. As the Moon dies away, you can move away from areas that feel best left behind. Focusing on healing, meditation, self-care, and nurturing one's spirit is essential during this Moon phase.

● The Full Moon: How it can affect your star sign

The Full Moon shines a light on areas that seek adjustment or healing in your life.

The Full Moon is a time to bring awareness into your spirit of the areas that seek resolution or adjustment. Over time, the past can create emotional blockages in your life. The Full Moon forms a sacred space to process sensitive emotions and release the past's hold on your spirit.

This lunar vibration brings awareness to your spirit of how your emotions affect your daily life. When the Moon is complete, your emotional awareness magnifies, and you feel things more intensely in your everyday life.

The Full Moon brings a chance to go over the inner terrain and connect with your intuition. She shines a light on areas that hold the most significant meaning in your life. This effect has a powerful impact on creativity, planning, and future life direction. Tuning in and listening to your gut instincts helps you strip away from areas that only cloud judgment and muddy your awareness.

Capricorn: The Full Moon focuses on your daily life and home environment. It helps restore your basic foundations, making you feel safe and secure. It offers fresh air for your creativity and can lead to important epiphanies about your future life direction. Expect a turning point or epiphany to improve interpersonal relationships. The Full Moon energizes communication and improves bonds in your life.

I use the 24-hour clock/military time.
Time set to Coordinated Universal Time Zone (UT±0)

I've noted Meteor Showers on the date they peak.

January

Sun	Mon	Tue	Wed	Thu	Fri	Sat
1	2	3	4	5	6	7
8	9	10	11	12	13	14
15	16	17	18	19	20	21
22	23	24	25	26	27	28
29	30	31				

New Moon

Wolf Moon

December/January

30 Friday

Something you have been developing for your life this year has reached fruition. It does bring a successful result into your life. It lands you in a new chapter that offers freedom, adventure, and possibility. The path ahead glimmers with refreshing options that nurture an extended time of expanding your world. It brings a broader picture of what is possible when you develop the borders of your life.

31 Saturday

An undercurrent of unique potential surrounds your life. Transformation sweeps in to encourage expansion. It brings an enriching chapter that sees you laying the groundwork for an exciting path forward in your life. It brings lighter energy and the freedom to chart a course towards happiness. It offers growth around your social life, and as the pace and rhythm of life pick up steam, you discover a clear path forward.

1 Sunday ~ New Year's Day, Venus conjunct Pluto 5:24

Venus, the ruler of love, offers an abundant landscape when conjunct with Pluto. The energy of transformation surrounds your life, enabling you to advance your romantic life. The future looks rosy as you land in a unique, exciting landscape that draws lighter energy into your romantic life. A vibrant and exciting influence sparks advancement around your personal goals. You attract a buzz of activity that promotes romance.

January

2 Monday ~ Mercury sextile Neptune 6:53

This sextile attracts free-flowing and creative ideas that help you place the cherry on this year's plans and aspirations. Good news brings a significant shift forward that teams you up with rising prospects. It offers an uptick of new options that have you feeling energized and ready to tackle new projects with a view toward advancement. You discover a unique opportunity that captures the essence of inspiration and enables you to build this year's plans.

3 Tuesday ~ Venus ingress Aquarius 2:06, Quadrantids Meteors runs Jan 1st – 5th

Exciting options let you set sail on a new adventure. It brings growth; it enables you to create fantastic progress as you develop your vision. It is a shift that brings a new leaf of potential. Your ability to clear the blocks that hold you back brings a time that activates a fresh chapter. It nurtures your life and connects you with other lively characters. It lets you soak up a glorious chapter of social engagement and harmony.

4 Wednesday ~ Venus sextile Jupiter 9:07

This sextile attracts warm and abundant energy into your social life. A dash of luck and good fortune combined with enriching conversations improve social bonds in your life. Your life enters a phase of growth when social opportunities emerge, which offer a chance to mingle with kindred spirits. It connects you with a compelling journey that enriches your life. It marks the beginning of a chapter of potential that is your ticket to a happy and fulfilled personal life.

5 Thursday ~ Sun trine Uranus 16:43

This Sun trine Uranus transit brings positive change and excitement into your world. An important decision cracks the code to improving your life. You pour your energy into an area that draws pleasing results. It connects with a social aspect that nurtures companionship. You discover a new role that brings well-being and harmony. It ends delays as life moves forward, bringing an expansive and liberating phase that rekindles inspiration.

January

6 Friday ~ Wolf Full Moon in Cancer 23:09

Healing under Cancer's Full Moon feels good for your soul. While you have known troubles before in your life, you have a remarkable ability to change, adapt and grow. It helps you discover a diamond in the rough as you unearth a journey of discovery that glitters with golden possibilities. Excitement ahead nurtures growth in your social life. It brings friendship and companionship. Getting involved in this environment draws an enriching time.

7 Saturday ~ Sun Conjunct Mercury 12:56

This conjunct bodes well for communication. Rising prospects draw insightful conversations that stimulate creativity and problem-solving mental energy. A richer life experience arrives to heal an aspect that has been out of alignment recently. It does help you release bottled-up emotions that have caused tension that limited your true potential. You enter an exciting time that facilitates warm expressions and heartfelt conversations.

8 Sunday ~ Mercury trine Uranus 23:22

Mercury forming a trine with Uranus brings flashes of insight; expect an epiphany as brilliance surrounds your thought processes today. Positive signs ahead give you a glimmer of insight into the path forward. You enter a transformational aspect that renews the potential possible. It brings a beautiful journey that promotes happiness. Difficulties fade away as you rekindle inspiration. A fantastic outlook ahead attracts optimism and joy.

January

9 Monday ~ Venus trine Mars 15:21

This week, Venus trine Mars raises your energy and brings a vibrant passion for life. Something unique and exciting tempts you out of your usual routine. It brings an environment ripe with blessings that lets you head to a long-held goal. You immerse yourself in an area worth your time, and life becomes brighter as you unpack new options that stir up the essence of manifestation. It nurtures a landscape that draws advancement into your situation.

10 Tuesday

Being open and receptive to change helps you weather storms and adapt and grow. It directs your attention to developing areas that let you move toward greener pastures. Personal growth attracts self-development, and this carries you towards rising prospects. It enables you to release the blocks and increases the drive to develop unique goals that enhance your abilities. As you expand your life into new areas, you enjoy a stream of possibilities that propel you onwards.

11 Wednesday

Making your goals a priority helps you discover a path that promotes growth, advancement, and progression. It lets you eliminate problems and focus on the most meaningful journey forward. A cycle of growth captures the essence of manifestation as it brings a shift towards new possibilities. It sees you working with your abilities and developing skills as you chart a course towards rising prospects.

12 Thursday ~ Mars turns direct at 20:54

With the planet Mars moving forward, your energy, passion, and drive return to full force. It helps you navigate a complex environment and develop solutions that offer a fresh start. You uncover confidential information that draws clarity and insight into your life. Exploring various avenues helps to establish your talents in a productive area. It lets you build a platform that takes your abilities to a new level. It extends your reach to a broader audience.

January

13 Friday ~ Sun sextile Neptune 14:11

Resources and support help you get busy manifesting your vision. Information arrives soon that helps progress your path forward. It brings the right time to begin working on your career goals. It enables you to build remarkable growth and prosperity; changes ahead extend your reach into a new area of possibility. It offers a carefree time that heightens creativity and brings new projects and assignments worthy of your attention.

14 Saturday

A shift forward brings a lovely boost to your world. It does highlight new options that encourage you to expand your horizons. You can create abundance by exploring all that life has to offer. A further possibility emerges that causes a great deal of excitement. It revolves around learning a new area, which creates a productive growth phase. You generate your leads and can go for gold. Fortune lights a shimmering path that makes you eager to begin a new journey.

15 Sunday ~ Venus square Uranus 1:21, Last Quarter Moon in Libra 2:12

A Venus Uranus square creates a need to balance and harmonize personal bonds while honoring your need for freedom and expression. Life holds a refreshing change. It opens a journey of liberation as new possibilities draw growth and expansion, lighting a path glittering with potential. It helps you shake off the heavy vibes and head towards an exciting time developing your world.

January

16 Monday ~ Martin Luther King Day

A lot of potential is heading your way. It brings a good time for taking on new assignments and developing projects. Optimism is a golden key that opens the path to new possibilities in your life. New opportunities spring to life and open a blossoming way forward in your life. It does bring a time of significant personal growth and advancement. Life offers new possibilities that help you navigate greener pastures.

17 Tuesday

Intuitive choices bring new possibilities into your life. It provides an essential phase of expansion, growth, and opportunity. Getting involved in creating a life of your making helps smooth over the rough edges and lets you set sail towards smoother sailing. Taking action is a positive step that nurtures your life from the ground up. You discover strength, courage, and conviction that propels you forward to new challenges.

18 Wednesday ~ Mercury turns direct at 13:12

Mercury is the messenger planet of communication, collaboration, and creative expression. Life becomes more manageable and flows more easily during Mercury's direct phase. News arrives, which sparks a path of growth, learning, and accomplishment. It kicks off a wonderful time that nurtures your abilities. Lighter energy is coming to lift your spirits. It brings new possibilities to the forefront of your life.

19 Thursday

You are moving to a pivotal time where you can create growth in your life. A side project ahead taps into innovative inclinations and offers room to promote your talents to a broader audience. Choices and decisions ahead shape a path that attracts rising prospects. It represents a new beginning that sweeps away the negativity and ushers in a pleasing result.

January

20 Friday ~ Sun ingress Aquarius 8:26

Your knack for creativity shines as you get busy and establish your gifts in an area worth your time. A potent mix of manifestation surrounds your life as you reveal new possibilities. It expands your circle of friends, and sharing companionship with others promotes well-being and happiness. Indeed, social events on the horizon land you in a refreshing environment.

21 Saturday ~ New Moon in Aquarius 20:54

You are going through a time of transition, and improving your life is a big theme that draws new possibilities into your life. Nurturing your goals attracts an exciting phase of potential. It lets you embrace life-affirming endeavors that restore happiness and attract new friends into your life. Rising confidence promotes expansion, and socializing with your broader circle delivers a wellspring of possibilities.

22 Sunday ~ Venus conjunct Saturn 22:12, Uranus turns direct 23:23
Chinese New Year (Rabbit)

The Chinese New Year heralds good luck and fortune. Rabbits are a symbol of growth and fertility. Ideas planted in fertile terrain will get a chance to blossom and grow. Significant changes ahead connect you with a prosperous time that offers development in your life. Being open to discovering new leads helps you find effective options circulating in the background. Being available to change is a catalyst for growth in your life.

January

23 Monday

You get a chance to develop a project that catches your interest. Manifesting happiness draws new possibilities that help you progress your life forward. A time of discovery looms overhead and links you up with options that enable you to build a path toward your dreams. Growing your abilities draws the knowledge to assist you with unlocking an enterprising area. Possibilities emerge that offer rising prospects for your life.

24 Tuesday

A great deal of potential surrounds your life. News arrives, which helps you move forward towards growth and advancement. It connects you with a phase of expansion that offers rising prospects that help you chart a course towards developing a lofty goal. Breaking up the stagnant patterns in your life opens pathways that offer bustling possibilities. An uptick of movement ahead facilitates progress and change.

25 Wednesday ~ Sun sextile Jupiter 1:30

In sextile with Jupiter, the Sun attracts a restless vibe that has you yearning to expand your life outwardly. You enter a social time that shines brightly with light and active engagement. Sharing thoughts with valued companions leads to discussing a new and vital assignment. This area is a pleasing showcase that enables you to take your talents to a broader audience. Rising confidence brings motivation and inspiration into your world.

26 Thursday

Setting positive intentions attracts an abundant landscape of possibility. Indeed, you can harness the power of manifestation and get busy developing new dreams that spark excitement in your life. Focusing on planning enables you to plot a tangible course forward. It marks a significant turning point that creates a robust foundation from which to grow life outwardly.

January

27 Friday ~ Venus ingress Pisces 2:29

News arrives, which enables you to achieve a purposeful push to expand your horizons. It opens the door to a social environment that promotes well-being and harmony. Indeed, happiness and optimism run right through the upcoming phase. The pace and rhythm of your life pick up speed, promoting opportunities that expand your circle of friends. You soon reveal a sunny aspect that attracts kinship.

28 Saturday ~ First Quarter Moon in Taurus 15:19

You head towards a breakthrough that brings a new chapter into your life. It gives you the green light to network, and these interactions engage proactively with your social life. Feeling in sync with your friends brings a valuable sense of connection into your life. It snags a time of lively discussions and group bonding sessions that feel right for your soul.

29 Sunday

Things are on the move for your life soon—new information fuels options to engage with your broader circle of friends. Heightening communication attracts invitations to mingle, promoting options that ensure you are kept busy—life blossoms into an enterprising path forward that connects with refreshing companions. There are a lot of newnesses arriving to bless your life.

February

Sun	Mon	Tue	Wed	Thu	Fri	Sat
			1	2	3	4
5	6	7	8	9	10	11
12	13	14	15	16	17	18
19	20	21	22	23	24	25
26	27	28				

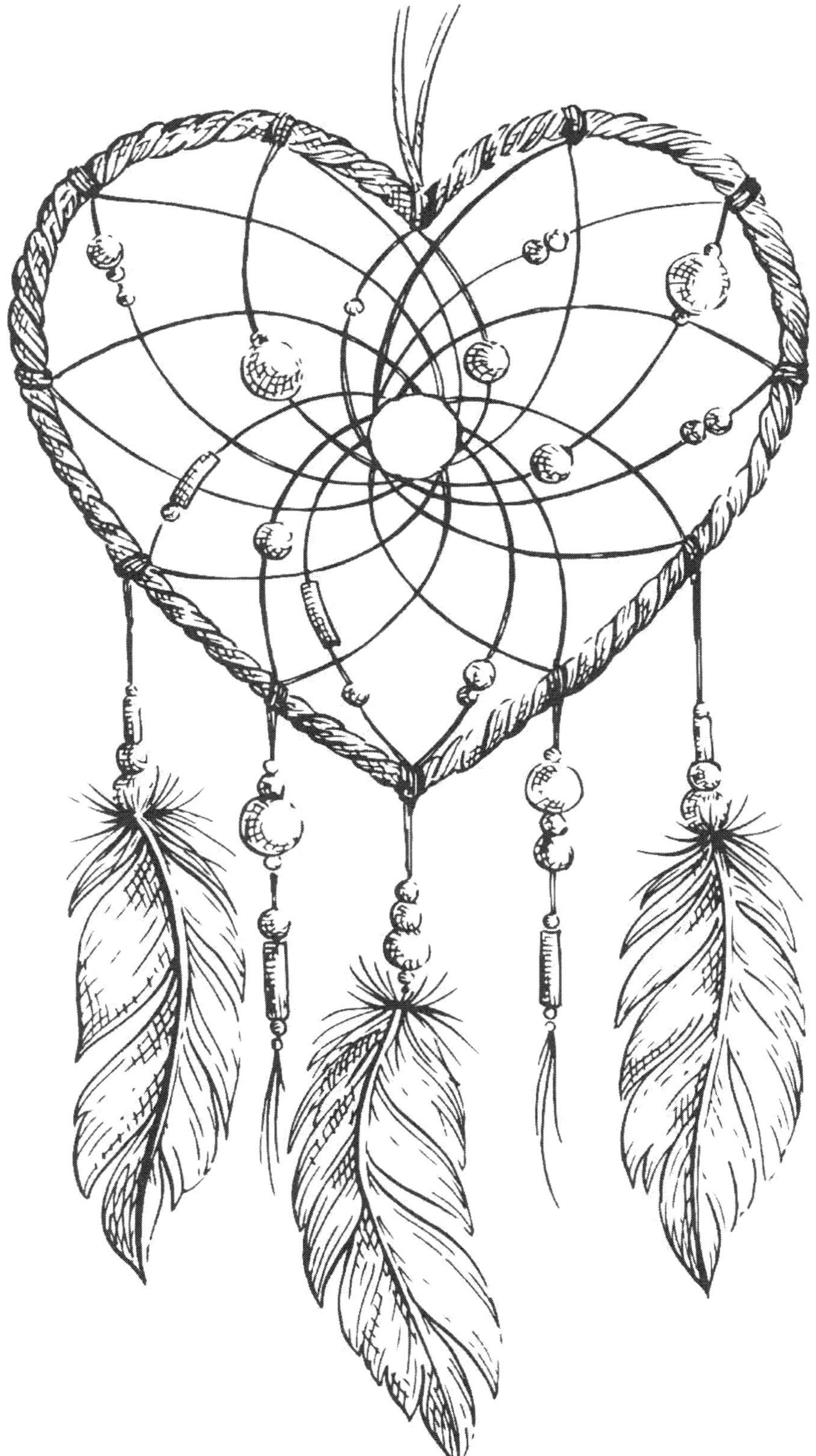

New Moon

Snow Moon

January/February

30 Monday ~ Sun trine Mars 1:45, Mercury trine Uranus 2:17
Mercury at Greatest Eastern Elongation: 25.0°W

If you feel caught in a holding pattern, rest assured that new opportunities soon get the ball rolling on developing a fresh chapter. It begins a positive trend that helps you grow as it brings possibilities that have you thinking expansively. It brings assignments that take your abilities to a broader audience. Innovative thinking and creative possibilities are handy aspects to help you strike gold.

31 Tuesday

Broadening your perception of what is possible helps you unearth leads that attract advancement. The more you nurture your creativity and refine your abilities, the more you engage with growing your life in an enterprising and exciting direction. Seeing positive results fuels inspiration and lets you progress towards unique goals. It positions you to achieve growth as you advance towards developing your skills.

1 Wednesday ~ Imbolc

A pathway opens, which brings opportunity knocking. It lets you enter an exciting time as you evolve and grow your vision to the next level. It connects with areas that deepen your skills and knowledge. Leaning into challenges draws extraordinary possibilities for growth and advancement. You discover an endeavor worth your time, and this helps you uncover a golden nugget worth developing.

2 Thursday~ Groundhog Day

Life brims with refreshing options that open the gate to a fresh chapter. Acting on a hunch promotes a golden return that unleashes a positive trend in your life. It sees your social circle becoming more connected, and this helps you establish grounded foundations that grow your life. It brings lively discussions and companionship to the forefront of your life. News arrives that gets a boost to your situation.

February

3 Friday

Your life is ripening with fresh possibilities that draw rising prospects into your life. It seems something new is waiting to blossom, and being open to growing your world in a new direction rewards a meaningful journey forward. There are opportunities to engage with your social circle. This heightening of social engagement brings an expressive path that focuses on deepening bonds with people who hold significance in your life.

4 Saturday ~ Sun square Uranus 2:50

This positive square offers rising creativity that cultivates a new approach. Taking a moment to process any unresolved emotions lingering around your energy draws pleasing results. It speaks of a choice ahead that marks the transition towards a happy chapter. Being in a more social environment resonates wonderfully with your spirit. It does bring stability and consistency into your life. It draws a situation with you exploring fresh ideas and engaging in entertaining discussions.

5 Sunday ~ Venus square Mars 3:28, Snow Full Moon in Leo 18:30

This square can cause challenges as a difference of opinion fosters tension and conflict. Flexible, understanding, and adaptive will help harmonize bonds and limit the disruption caused by Venus facing Mars at a harsh angle. Being willing to compromise will improve the foundations and limit the disruption in your life.

FEBRUARY

6 Monday ~ Mercury sextile Neptune 18:27

Rational thinking and dreams align in this sextile. You see rising creativity and analytical thinking promoting epiphanies that count. This cosmic alignment helps your dreams become a reality as structured backing behind your vision offers tangible results. It brings a busy time of sifting and sorting through potential options. Laying the groundwork secures foundations that are ripe for growth. Changes ahead help you reach a bright path onward.

7 Tuesday

You discover new opportunities in life that shower over into your situation, which offer a rich and generous time to work with your creativity. It brings an extended time of growth which heightens the sense of security in your life as you head towards transformation on many levels. A journey of rejuvenation brings an open road of possibility that tempts you forward. It helps you lay stable foundations that feel grounded and complete.

8 Wednesday ~ Venus sextile Uranus 5:28

Spontaneity, fun, and fresh adventures rule your social life with this engaging sextile. Heightened opportunities ahead lead to a progressive phase of social engagement. It brings extra support and a sense of connection to your door. It lets you chart a course towards an enriching chapter that ushers in laughter, music, and lively discussions. It brings thoughtful dialogue and helpful advice to the forefront of your world; in this fertile ground, creativity blossoms.

9 Thursday

The tides turn in your favor as a lucky break brings increasing opportunities. It cracks open a journey that promotes kinship and connection within your social circle. Confidence rises as opportunities to mingle draw lighter energy into your life. Exploring social opportunities connects you with an expansive phase that brings an invitation to your door. Unique options ahead offer a journey of discovery.

FEBRUARY

10 Friday ~ Mercury conjunct Pluto 17:16

Today's conjunct between Mercury and Pluto offers intense curiosity to delve a little deeper into life's mysteries. As you work on improving your circumstances, you sense that something big is around the corner. Lighter energy brings strength and creative power that cultivates inspiring ideas. A meticulous approach to improving your circumstances brings opportunities that create a bridge to a bright chapter. It emphasizes self-expression, identity, and creativity.

11 Saturday ~ Mercury ingress Aquarius 11:22

A busy aspect brings a sense of purpose as you move forward and engage with life proactively. A whirlwind of activity overhead connects you with social possibilities. Manifesting happiness is on the agenda as you share thoughtful conversations and find balance and harmony rising. Surprise news lands and brings an invitation to attend a gathering shared with friends. It offers an outlet for your restless energy that fuels spirited discussions.

12 Sunday

A sunny aspect flings open some attractive new possibilities in your life. Good luck blooms as you channel your energy into a journey that inspires you creatively. A wellspring of magic courses through your situation, bringing improving circumstances. A happy time shared with friends resonates with inspiration and happiness. It releases the heaviness and opens a growth path in your social life.

FEBRUARY

13 Monday ~ Last Quarter Moon in Scorpio 16:01

Momentum gathers as you redefine your life's constructs by being open and flexible to new people and environments. It lets you gain a deeper understanding of your natural strengths and talents. Renewal and rejuvenation is a theme that resonates in your world as you connect with friends who offer a supportive vibe. Life moves towards a social aspect that brings a vibrant landscape to explore.

14 Tuesday ~ Valentine's Day

Today nurtures romance and leads to a happy occasion that fuels inspiration. It attracts lively discussions, and amid these stimulating conversations, you deepen a bond that offers room to grow into a meaningful journey forward. Sharing this day with another connects you with an exciting and happy aspect that brings a wellspring of abundance into your life. It sparks a lively and social time that promotes a thoughtful path forward in your romantic life.

15 Wednesday ~ Venus conjunct Neptune 12:25

Venus joins forces with Neptune, and your love life takes on a dreamy quality as you engage in fanciful thoughts and contemplation. The desire moves into unlimited imagination as you think about the future, intending to nurture romance in your life. It helps you reawaken to the vibrant landscape of potential that surrounds your life. It lights a journey filled with hopes, dreams, and possibilities.

16 Thursday ~ Saturn conjunct Sun 16:48

Saturn connects with the Sun to blaze a trail towards developing your goals. Getting serious about limiting distractions and cultivating discipline, concentration, and order will help you nail progress in your working life. Gaining traction on improving security in your world will bring a valuable sense of achievement and accomplishment to your door. It positions you correctly to achieve growth and expand your world.

February

17 Friday

News arrives that offers an exciting change. A snap decision cracks the code to a vibrant landscape. Life picks up steam, bringing new flavors and possibilities that inspire growth. Broadening horizons offers room to grow a path that sees potential blossoming. Being open to new leads encourages creative thinking. It lets you come up with a winning destination. It offers an enterprising approach that develops new goals.

18 Saturday ~ Mercury sextile Jupiter 2:13, Sun ingress Pisces 22:30

The Mercury Jupiter aspect creates harmony between both planets. It sparks rising curiosity, questioning, and fresh ideas. As creativity heightens, it brings an epiphany that provides an open road of possibility. Stirring the pot of manifestation brings impressive results to your door. Being available to change brings a time of growth and prosperity that restores equilibrium and gives a more stable basis to the foundations in your life.

19 Sunday ~ Venus sextile Pluto 17:04

Today's Venus and Pluto alignment offers depth and insight into your thought processes. It helps you dig a little deeper and discover what drives your passion. Thinking about the areas that hold the most significant meaning in your life can be helpful on many levels. It weeds out the sites no longer a good fit for your life by letting you see the most meaningful aspects of your world. Moving in alignment with the person you are becoming nurtures inspiration and passion.

February

20 Monday ~ Presidents' Day. New Moon in Pisces 7:08, Venus ingress Aries 7:52

Today shows fortune shining in your life as you transition towards a cheerful chapter that sees the sun beaming overhead. You enter an extended time that promotes growth in your social life, seeing you meet new friends and share with engaging companions. It is a fruitful time that attracts opportunities not previously encountered. It begins a path of expanding options that ushers in change.

21 Tuesday ~ Shrove Tuesday (Mardi Gras), Mercury square Uranus 22:22

Original thinking, creative brainstorming, and insightful epiphanies are the order of the day as Mercury squares off against Uranus today. New ideas, curiosity, and thirst for knowledge will rise as you open your life up to developing unique areas that spark your interest. Re-examining goals and researching hold you in a good position as you turn the corner and head towards growth. Developing your ideas brings developments that offer advancement.

22 Wednesday ~ Ash Wednesday, Lent Begins, Mercury trine Mars 20:14

A Mercury trine Mars aspect attracts a restless vibe. This cosmic alignment leaves you feeling spontaneous and ready for new adventures today. It begins a bustling phase of developing your social life. This expansion offers an active and busy time that feels refreshing and therapeutic for your spirit. Communication arrives that shines the light around deepening friendships. An opportunity for collaboration offers growth and a sense of kinship.

23 Thursday

Beautiful symmetry is ahead as you spot signs guiding the path towards greater happiness and abundance. Enriching your life is a ticket for success as you soon see tangible progress fuelling more fantastic inspiration. It places you in the box seat to develop projects that grow your vision and improve the potential possible in your world. Chasing expansion hits a sweet note as you head towards a productive time.

FEBRUARY

24 Friday

Changes help reboot your life as it brings ample opportunity to connect with friends. It opens a journey of growing your world as you share experiences and thoughts with others. It extends life to a broader range of possibilities that promote lively conversations which offer social engagement and happiness. It ushers in a time of change and inspiration that brings goodness to the top of your social life.

25 Saturday

A thoughtful approach brings happiness and abundance into your personal life. It brings changes that align you towards deepening romance and sharing a journey with another. You beautifully orient your life towards deepening romance, passion, and connection. Being adaptable and flexible nurture stable foundations and enable you to forge a rewarding path forward for your private life.

26 Sunday

Information ahead helps build more grounded foundations in your life. You discover an area that adds fuel to your emotional tank. Life takes on a lighter hue as blossoming activity attracts new options. It helps you develop a journey that offers room to grow into a unique path forward. Indeed, it enables you to express your talents creatively and effectively to achieve growth.

March

Sun	Mon	Tue	Wed	Thu	Fri	Sat
			1	2	3	4
5	6	7	8	9	10	11
12	13	14	15	16	17	18
19	20	21	22	23	24	25
26	27	28	29	30	31	

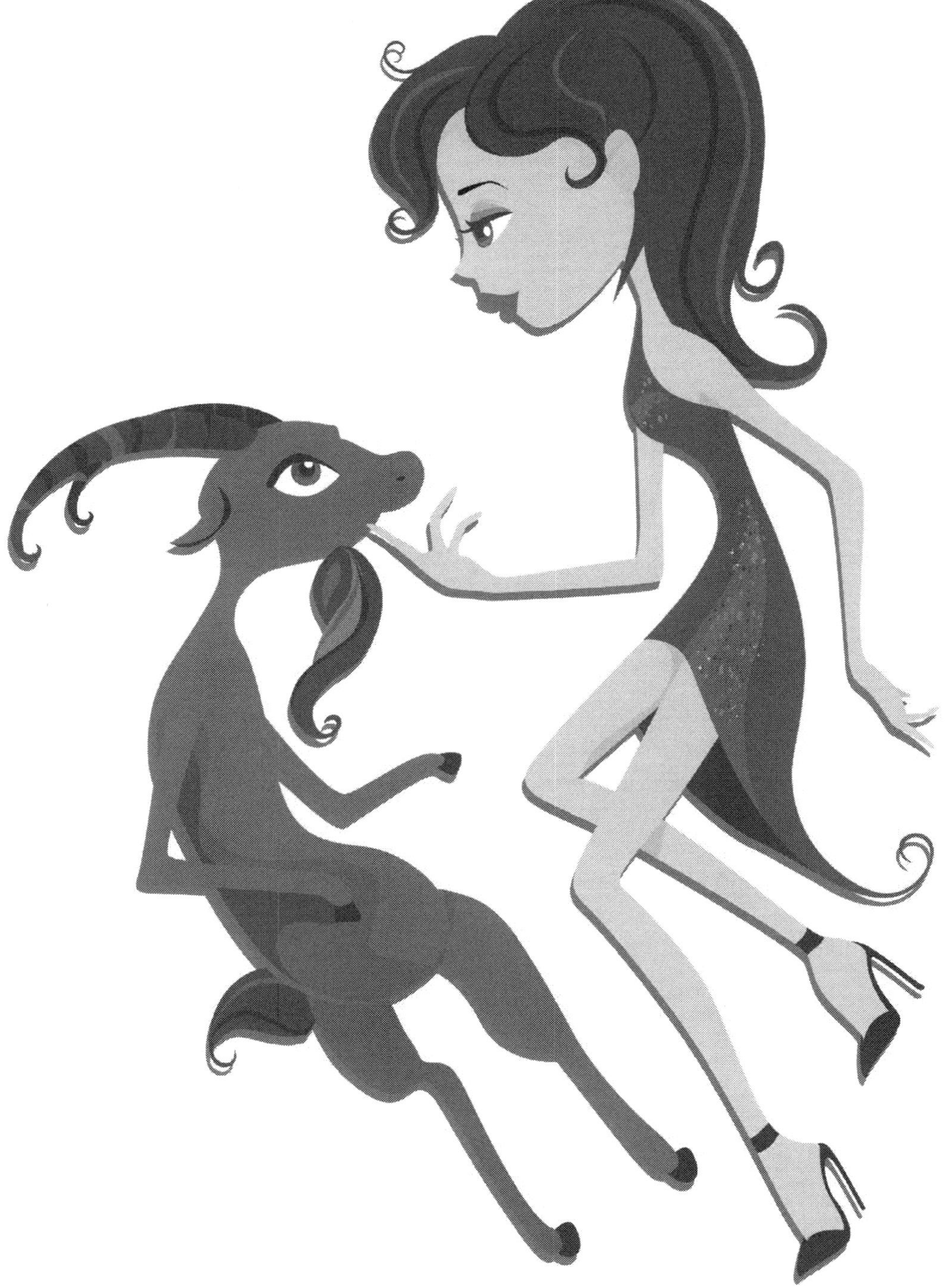

New Moon

Worm Moon

February/March

27 Monday ~ First Quarter Moon in Gemini 8:06

Surprise news shifts your focus towards developing a new area. An exciting option emerges, which provides you with a fantastic direction. It gives you a path to channel your excess energy into growing. You discover a fascinating journey that deepens your knowledge and expands your skills. It connects you with kindred spirits and promotes social engagement, leading to greater happiness in your life.

28 Tuesday

You benefit from opportunities ahead as they link up with a refreshing time that encourages growth, advancement, and rising prospects. Learning a new area is a winning formula that deepens your knowledge and refines your skills. It kicks off a phase of inspiration as you cast a light on your career path and see new possibilities which promote growth. It draws an active time of working with your abilities.

1 Wednesday

Being ethical and righteous makes you responsible for your actions and choices. Being discerning and accountable, harness the energy of karma to your advantage. Listening to your intuition help you make fair and just decisions. You move on with your life and journey in alignment with your core feelings. It opens up options for growth in your career, and a new path beckons, offering advancement in your life.

2 Thursday ~ Venus conjunct Jupiter 17:35, Mercury conjunct Saturn 14:34, Mercury ingress Pisces 22:49

Today's Venus conjunct Jupiter aspect is a positive sign for your social life. Expect an upward trend as rising prospects draw communication and invitations to mingle. News arrives, which draws a productive time as it connects you with a phase of social engagement. A situation you become involved with begins to move forward, attracting expansion and growth.

March

3 Friday

You think about potential changes for your life and share thoughtful discussions before making any decisions. It prompts you to reassess your life and develop a connected framework to grow your goals. Listening to advice and sharing thoughts with your tribe brings rising prospects into your world. Magic course through your life, helping new goals blossom. You see the possibilities and head towards your dreams.

4 Saturday

Your life blossoms as you deepen a love connection and share dreams and goals with an insightful companion. Open and authentic communication creates a powerful journey forward in your romantic life. Your ideas and inspiration make the stepping stones that offer a brighter future for your life. You find dreams are within reach as you harness the inspiration and creativity within your spirit.

5 Sunday

Beautiful symmetry is coming into your life which helps nurture grounded foundations. It brings a highly creative and expressive time that enables you to set sail on a voyage of your creation. Working with your creativity offers happiness and self-improvement, guiding you towards growing your talents. Extending your reach and listening to your instincts opens a journey that grows a positive chapter in your life.

March

6 Monday ~ Purim (Begins at sundown), Sun sextile Uranus 13:41

This sextile heightens creativity and self-expression. You discover a new approach that boosts productivity and offers efficiency in your daily life. Change and discovery add a spontaneous element today. Anything could crop up to provide you with a sign of newfound inspiration. It offers you the chance to share your talents with a broader audience. It opens your world up to new possibilities that light a path forward towards an abundant landscape.

7 Tuesday ~ Worm Full Moon in Virgo 12:40 Purim (Ends at sunset), Saturn ingress Pisces 13:03

The planet Saturn moving into Pisces is a significant shift. This change of the Saturnian guards highlights the need for spiritual healing. It emphasizes finding meaning in your daily life and growing a solid spiritual basis to help you ride out any turbulence in your life. Refining your spiritual life takes you on a comprehensive journey; it encompasses an extended time of increasing your life in new directions. It ultimately brings a better sense of purpose into your world.

8 Wednesday

Changes ahead bring the opportunity to grow your life in a meaningful area. It offers an enriching chapter that sees you working with your skills and developing your abilities as you chart a course towards growth. Fine-tuning your vision enables you to cut away from areas that fail to bear fruit. Developing an effective plan helps you make strides towards building new endeavors that yield a strong sense of enrichment and happiness.

9 Thursday

As you rush forward and develop critical areas of your life, you see opportunities for growth that nurture rising prospects. A fast-paced environment draws advancement into your life. Refining your skills and cultivating knowledge, crack the code to a bright chapter. You take disciplined action as you have the drive and perseverance to nail developing your dreams.

MARCH

10 Friday

Setting your sights on opening your world up to new people and possibilities can help encourage growth in other areas. You land gently in an environment that progresses life forward. You break fresh ground when a communication arrives from someone who has been out of the loop lately. Nurturing social connections bring a busy time of advancing life forward. It marks a time of building grounded foundations that restore equilibrium and balance to your life.

11 Saturday ~ Venus sextile Mars 15:04, Mercury sextile Uranus 21:04

Venus has your back today and draws social engagement into your life. Keeping the bar raised does offer long-term benefits. It helps you sift and sort the path ahead and move away from areas that fail to reach fruition. A whirlwind of activity overhead draws new options into your life. It ushers in an essential phase of active involvement with your social life. Life blossoms with opportunities, and you soon build stable foundations in your home life.

12 Sunday

It is quiet before a significant shift forward occurs in your life. Gaining traction on achieving your goals becomes a strong focus. You keep forging ahead until you accomplish the rightful outcome. Persisting on this course and building new foundations in your life facilitates expansion, which keeps motivation humming. Serendipitous changes give you glimmers of hope that things are ready to turn a corner.

MARCH

13 Monday

You use innovative techniques and intuitive intelligence to obtain your objectives. You explore pathways in your life which improve circumstances and grow your world. You deepen your knowledge by immersing yourself in studies that offer wisdom, guidance, and advancement. Your dedication to improving life draw dividends as you pivot away from hurdles and channel your energy into developing an essential objective.

14 Tuesday

Significant change arrives to bring a chapter that empowers growth and enriches your life. It does get a lofty goal that sets your sights on achieving abundance in your romantic life. The power of manifestation lights the way forward towards transformation. It lets you open the floodgates to a happy chapter as you create space to develop your dreams and grow your world in a meaningful direction. Expanding the boundaries of your life draws transformation and happiness.

15 Wednesday ~ Last Q Moon in Sagittarius 2:08, Sun conjunct Neptune 23:39

You may feel sensitivities rising today as the Sun links up with Neptune in the sign of Pisces today. Intuition is sparking; you can trust your gut instincts to guide you correctly when you reveal curious information that triggers your emotions. It marks a time of rejuvenation that helps you sweep away areas that are no longer relevant. It sets in motion the essence of manifestation that gently shifts your focus toward developing the goals you have in mind.

16 Thursday ~ Mercury conjunct Neptune 17:13, Sun square Mars 18:09, Venus square Pluto 19:58, Venus ingress Taurus 22:31

Today, you may feel chaotic and under pressure as a great deal of cosmic energy disrupts stability in your life. Expect intensity as the Sun square Mars alignment may leave you feeling tense and hot under the collar. Creative expression and taking time to make yourself a priority will be beneficial in releasing frustrations and any heavy energy clinging to your spirit.

MARCH

17 Friday ~ St Patrick's Day. Mercury square Mars 4:48, Sun conjunct Mercury 10:45, Venus sextile Saturn 20:25

Today, Venus sextile Saturn promotes cooperation and offers the chance to join a joint project. Exploring leads and researching options helps you come up with a winning trajectory. It provides you with an approach that lets you chase your vision for future growth. You soon build stable foundations that heighten the security in your life. You make your mark on developing goals in your life.

18 Saturday

Life turns a corner when communication reveals an exciting possibility for your social life. You attract an invitation that broadens the borders of your world as you enter a supportive environment that nurtures stability. It brings a time of cultivating dreams and sharing thoughtful discussions with friends. Rekindling vitality attracts possibilities to develop new projects as you expand your horizons.

19 Sunday ~ Mercury ingress Aries 4:22

You crack the code to a bright chapter when revealing information that opens up prospects. It offers a lush environment from which to chase developing dreams. It links you with kindred spirits, which draws heightened opportunities to mingle with your circle of friends. Something newsworthy filters down the gossip line, bringing new information to light. It attracts a happy time deepening ties and enjoying shared moments with friends.

March

20 Monday ~ Sun sextile Pluto 20:12, Sun ingress Aries 21:20, Ostara/Spring Equinox 21:25

Important career news reaches your inbox and translates into an opportunity worth considering. Getting involved in developing the prospects surrounding your life lets you take a proactive role in guiding your path forward. Immersing yourself in a challenging but rewarding area invigorates your spirit. An appealing approach calls your name and gets life on track to progress.

21 Tuesday ~ New Moon in Pisces 17:22

You charge ahead towards more outstanding achievements by planning the path and setting intentions during the New Moon phase. You can make intelligent decisions and wise choices. Even when things don't turn out as predicted, your ability to weather storms and navigate around hurdles is empowering. You have a bright mind that comes up with solutions. A time of happiness is the icing on the cake as you celebrate life on a large scale.

22 Wednesday ~ Ramadan Begins

Life is ripe with potential and ready to blossom. It brings choices and decisions that promote rapid expansion as you shift your focus toward developing your career path. Mapping out long-term goals becomes a turning point that enables you to chase your vision and gain traction on improving circumstances. It lets you use your talents to stunning effect as you head towards change. It is a time that offers opportunities for growth and expansion.

23 Thursday ~ Pluto ingress Aquarius 8:42

Exploring options helps you extend your reach into a new area worth your time. You can reclaim your goals and work towards your vision of a happy and stable career path by being proactive and growing your world outwardly. Inspiring progress leaves you optimistic as you enter a fast-moving environment that offers greater productivity and success. It becomes the gateway from which you deepen your knowledge and advance your skills.

MARCH

24 Friday

Information ahead enables you to progress your vision. Releasing blocks creates space to nurture your creativity. It does draw new possibilities into your life. It brings the essence of manifestation. Gaining traction on achieving your goals becomes a strong focus. Persisting on this course and building new foundations in your life facilitates expansion. Serendipitous changes give you glimmers of hope that things are ready to turn a corner.

25 Saturday ~ Mars ingress Cancer 11:36

A breakthrough ahead rains unique potential in your life. It creates space to focus on developing your skills. You release the past as you shake off the heavy vibrations that have dialed in your creativity. Tapping into your wildest instincts helps you carve out a journey that speaks to your soul. It liberates the areas of creativity, passion, and inspiration. A far-flung destination comes into view, and you soon become busy building a bridge towards a brighter future.

26 Sunday

A healthy dose of optimism lights the path forward as information comes to light that helps crack the code to a brighter chapter. Your willingness to explore possibilities helps you discover unique options that facilitate advancement. A rebellious and freedom-loving journey reveals an exciting aspect that connects you with kindred spirits. It lets you touch down a path that promotes the development of new projects.

March

27 Monday

You discover helpful options which create a golden triangle of possibility. It brings luck, improvement, and security. Gathering your resources, you are open to a time of learning and refinement that shines on your skills. It gets the ball rolling on upgrading your career path, letting you take advantage of incoming opportunities that offer rising prospects. Advancement is coming, bringing a fertile environment from which to grow your life.

28 Tuesday ~ Mercury conjunct Jupiter 6:49

This astrological conjunct is perfect for brainstorming as ideas are big and expressive under this planetary influence. You connect with a journey that opens new pathways and possibilities in your world. Advancing your life into unique areas takes you towards growth and rising prospects. It connects you with kindred spirits who share similar values. Nurturing your dreams draws results as you get busy stirring the energy of manifestation to achieve your goals.

29 Wednesday ~ First Quarter Moon in Cancer 2:32

Growth and learning ahead create a strong foundation that brings new options to your table. Sifting and sorting through these possibilities lets you uncover a journey that offers room to elevate your talents and extend your reach into a new area. It has you working on larger goals. It brings a venture that captures your interest. This area allows you to develop an endeavor that inspires your mind. It is a good time when you take steps toward progressing your goals.

30 Thursday ~ Mars trine Saturn 19:03, Venus conjunct Uranus 22:25

Mars forms a trine with Saturn today to give your working life wings. Hard work, dedication, and perseverance improve the day-to-day foundations of your life. Venus teams up with Uranus to add a dash of spontaneity to your social/personal life. As you embark on a new adventure, staying true to yourself will keep you aligned with the person you are becoming. You land in an engaging environment that opens a beautiful journey forward in your life.

April

Sun	Mon	Tue	Wed	Thu	Fri	Sat
						1
2	3	4	5	6	7	8
9	10	11	12	13	14	15
16	17	18	19	20	21	22
23	24	25	26	27	28	29
30						

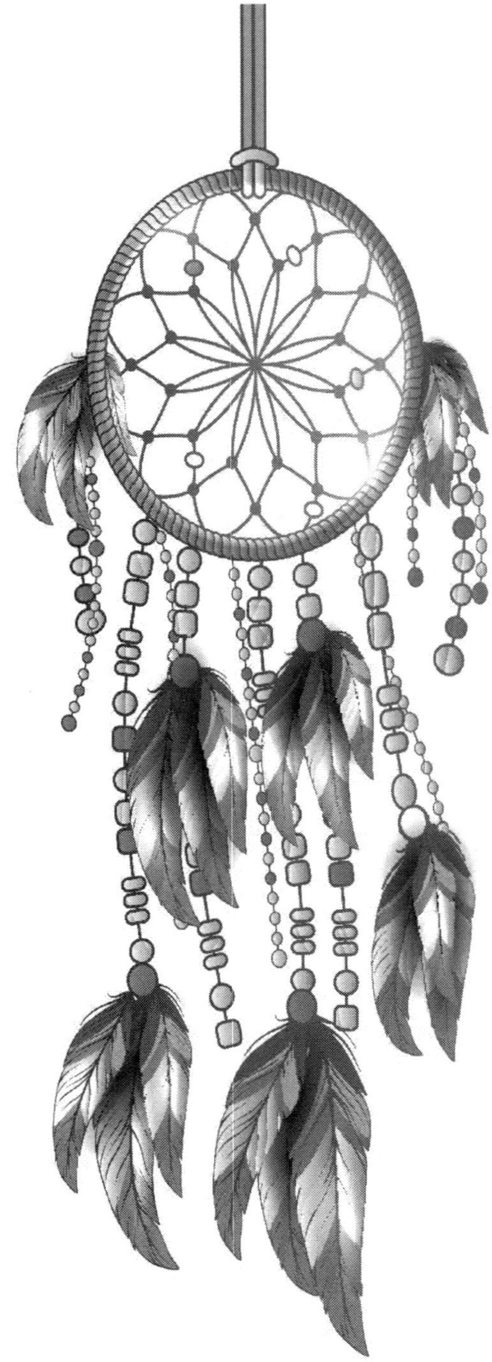

New Moon

Pink Moon

March/April

31 Friday

You enter a higher energy time that brings social engagement and support. It opens the floodgates to a happy time that emphasizes developing social ties. It gets a chance to unwind with kindred folk and relax in an ambient and engaging environment. Revealing new horizons in your life have you dreaming big about the possibilities. It gives you the green light to expand your life and nurture romance and magic.

1 Saturday ~ All Fools/April Fool's Day

Your social life moves from strength to strength as you develop new friendships and nurture companionship. Lightness and momentum return and help you reclaim vitality as you step out on a journey that grows into an inspiring path forward. You open a fresh chapter of your book of life that blossoms into a meaningful direction. Soul-expanding conversations add a reflective element that offers wisdom and grace.

2 Sunday ~ Palm Sunday.

Improvements are bound for your life as you benefit significantly from events on the horizon. You no longer feel like you are treading water as you sail toward new adventures. It offers a fresh start that improves stability and happiness. The tide turns in your favor, enabling choices and decisions to trigger a path that takes you towards rising prospects. It draws a replenishing vibe that brings renewal and rejuvenation.

April

3 Monday ~ Mercury ingress Taurus 16:20

Making informed choices helps you ascertain the correct journey forward for your working life. It brings a time that grows your abilities, enabling you to achieve maximum results—strategizing and planning harness the energy of focused intention to place you at a considerable advantage. It marks a shift forward that takes your goals to the next level. Branching out brings valuable results and advancement to your career path.

4 Tuesday

Hidden messages appear in your everyday life, and being conscious of the signs and symbols surrounding your world helps you discover a trail worth developing. It connects you with like-minded people who support and nurture thoughtful discussions. Indeed, life gathers momentum as you deepen the bond with a caring companion who enriches your life. It attracts a vibrant and exciting journey forward.

5 Wednesday ~ Passover (begins at sunset), Mercury sextile Saturn 16:18

With Mercury in sextile with Saturn, communication skills are rising. Enhanced clarity and mental insight help you understand more significant concepts, thought processes, and ideas with ease today. This cosmic enhancement enables you to step beyond traditional or repetitive learning and take your studies/working life to the next level. It helps you rise to the challenge and pole vault successfully over hump day. Confidence is increasing, enabling you to upgrade your working life and meet any demands on the to-do list.

6 Thursday ~ Lent Ends. Pink Full Moon in Libra 4:37

You spend time in a supportive and nurturing environment. Events align to nourish your soul and expand the borders of your world. It illustrates a lively discussion time that offers an open road to potential. There will be a chance to plan a trip away, something to work on to bring a goal into focus. Your willingness to open the door to new possibilities draws a pleasing result for your life.

APRIL

7 Friday ~ Good Friday, Venus sextile Neptune 17: 59

Today's planetary alignment offers a mindful, spiritual aspect that is in keeping with the spirit of Easter. Venus sends loving beams into your home and family life, harmonizing bonds and drawing the essence of rejuvenation and renewal. It sweeps good fortune into your life, lifts your spirits, and helps you chart a course towards nurturing a prosperous foundation around your home life. It offers a progressive phase that improves security in your world.

8 Saturday ~ Mercury sextile Mars 6:23

A sextile between Mercury and Mars sharpens cognitive abilities today. Mental clarity is on the rise, giving you valuable insight into the path ahead. It gives you an increased sense of motivation that provides an influx of inspiration. Beautiful changes attract the type of possibilities that offer growth and stability. A promising phase of good luck facilitates a happy trend in your life. It helps you expand your horizons and enjoy life.

9 Sunday ~Easter Sunday

Life showers a double dose of goodness over your situation. It brings a social aspect that offers entertaining discussions and a lively and vibrant atmosphere. A sense of celebration hangs in the air as you get busy catching up with friends and loved ones. Nurturing grounded foundations offers a boost that stabilizes and restores well-being and harmony. It lights a path forward to improving home and family life.

April

10 Monday

A surge of optimism opens the window to a brighter chapter. It illuminates a lighter environment that helps you craft a journey towards an inspiring goal. You discover plenty to celebrate as you set off in a new direction. Releasing the outworn energy dissolves sensitive areas. It creates space for a new life cycle that draws refreshing options. It provides an avenue that advances your skills. It ushers in a dynamic and progressive time.

11 Tuesday ~ Venus ingress Gemini 4:43, Venus trine Pluto 10:14, Sun Conjunct Jupiter 22:07, Mercury at Greatest Elong 19.5E

You can create abundance by exploring all that life has to offer. A further possibility emerges that causes a great deal of excitement. It revolves around learning a new area, which creates a productive growth phase. You generate your leads and can go for gold. It ends delays as you soon find heartening progress lights the path forward. Working on your craft brings fantastic results.

12 Wednesday

You get a leg up to a new area that offers an assignment that grows your skills. Being open to new opportunities facilitates change that opens life to an exciting flavor. You achieve a handsome reward by being open to new possibilities. It brings the news that lights a promising path toward growth. Taking on a new area draws a pleasing result. It rekindles inspiration and gets you busy working on a passion project that uses your talents to improve life.

13 Thursday ~ Passover (ends at sunset), Last Quarter Moon in Capricorn 9:11

Setting the bar higher brings a pleasing result. It helps you break past limitations and dive into an empowering phase of career growth. You build a bridge towards your vision by planning, preparing, and working towards your vision for future growth. Researching a unique area helps cultivate your talents and advance your skills. You stretch past your comfort zone and explore an exciting destination that calls your name.

April

14 Friday ~ Orthodox Good Friday, Venus square Saturn 16:38

A Venus square Saturn encourages taking a personal inventory of meaningful areas in your life. Shining a more intensive light on interpersonal situations in your social life helps you see the truth and eliminate outworn regions. Set firm boundaries if a drama llama is in your circle of friends. Being clear about things enables you to eliminate toxic influences that limit you from reaching your highest trajectory.

15 Saturday

Significant changes draw a breakthrough. It opens an inspiring time of connecting more often with friends. You get the wind back in your sails, and this sees inspiration humming along at a good clip. Life revs up with renewed possibilities, and this helps you open your world to new opportunities. It rules a journey of increasing expansion and harmony that opens a beautiful path forward for your life.

16 Sunday ~ Orthodox Easter

This time of rejuvenation is therapeutic and helpful. Removing outworn energy enables you to reclaim essential aspects of your nature. It promotes renewal and allows you to transition to an area that brings peace and balance into your surroundings. You tap into a journey that nourishes your life on many levels. It marks a significant turning point that helps you unpack rising prospects.

APRIL

17 Monday

Being open to change and exploring possibilities for your life helps you emerge from a quiet time and head towards growth. Pushing back the barriers lets you create tracks on growing your life and developing a journey that holds significant meaning to you. You can trust your instincts as you chase your dreams and forge a path forward. An area you promote developing offers exciting prospects for your career path.

18 Tuesday

You soon touch down an exciting path that develops your talents into a new area. It opens uncharted territory as you discover a gateway forward that grows your abilities. Expansion around your life promotes new goals and dreams. Life aligns favorably to upgrade your skills and develop your talents. Being open to change initiates a progression, growth, and evolution phase that offers an active and productive environment.

19 Wednesday

Preparation, planning, and strategizing provide you with critical elements that grow the potential possible in your world. It lets you come out as a winner as you embark on extending your life in a new direction. The conditions to grow your career path are ripening and bringing new possibilities into your life for a reason. It is a challenging environment on many levels, as it does take you out of your comfort zone, but the results are worthwhile

20 Thursday ~ Ramadan Ends, New Moon in Taurus 4:12, Hybrid Solar Eclipse, Sun ingress Taurus 8:09, Sun square Pluto 16:26

The Sun square Pluto aspect draws renewal and rejuvenation. Pluto charts a course towards transformation and offers a highly creative part that lights the way forward towards improving your circumstances. The Sun contributes to golden beings that offer harmony, transcendence, and rising prospects. This planetary combo elevates creative inclinations due to a New Moon.

APRIL

21 Friday ~ Mercury turns Retrograde in Taurus at 8:34

Mercury plays havoc with interpersonal bonds and can send communication haywire during its retrograde phase. Buckle up; it will be a bumpy ride as your social life goes on a Mercury-driven rollercoaster. If someone's contact triggers an emotional aspect, be mindful that this planetary phase is best with a balanced and understanding approach. As you navigate forward, focusing on being adaptable will give you a solid basis to stabilize personal bonds.

22 Saturday ~ Earth Day, Lyrids Meteor Shower from April 16th -25th

A social aspect lifts the lid on new options in your life. It opens a fortunate trend that blends with your ideas of future growth. It offers a busy time that connects with stable foundations as a positive influence brings a lively environment that nurtures thoughtful discussions. It creates a heightened sense of security that promotes balance and a grounded platform from which to grow your life.

23 Sunday

Fortune aligns to bring a new source of happiness into your life. You can expect developments that enable improvement in your social life. It promotes bonding sessions in a relaxed and ambient environment shared with friends. An invitation ahead lightens the atmosphere and brings thoughtful exchanges and discussions to the forefront of your life. It helps you chart a course towards a stable and supportive landscape.

APRIL

24 Monday ~ Mercury sextile Mars 3:22

Quick reflexes enable you to spot the diamond in the rough. The Mercury sextile with Mars offers new leads. A boost of good news arrives, which lets you hit a professional peak as you get a lucky break that elevates career prospects. Being open to new possibilities helps you chart a course towards success. Encouraging information brings a bonus into your world as it restores inspiration and attracts motivation to grow your world.

25 Tuesday ~ Sun sextile Saturn 10:47

Today's sextile brings opportunities that light a path forward. It illuminates fantastic potential that enables you to improve your circumstances. Change is ahead and brings advancements to your life. Setting aspirations help aid the flow of manifestation into your world. It gives you a chance to sharpen your talents and advance towards a new enterprise that offers room to grow your skillset. New options bring an opportunity to develop leads that offer rising prospects.

26 Wednesday

Improvements ahead elevate the potential possible. It brings a rising aspect into your life that helps you chart a course towards developing your skills in a new area. You follow a trail that cultivates greater security and advancement in your life. It brings a time of resourceful planning, research, and learning ahead. Your talents take center stage, which puts the shine on advancing your abilities as you extend your reach into a unique area worth your time.

27 Thursday ~ First Quarter Moon in Leo 21:20

Notable changes ahead highlight a journey of growth and progression in your life. As complications fade away, it releases outworn energy, bringing a healing vibration that offers sunshine to your world. Being discerning and selective brings a gemstone into your life. You spot a diamond in the rough, and polishing your talents enables you to make the most of this opportunity. A refreshing change brings a peak season for innovation, expansion, and good fortune.

APRIL

28 Friday

Information ahead jumpstarts growth in your life. It opens pathways that see you engaging in developing hobbies and interests. It draws a busy time of working with your skills and advancing your abilities in a new area. You land in a dynamic environment that attracts new options as you head towards a productive time that grows your world. It opens a journey that shows fantastic promise and potential.

29 Saturday ~ Mars sextile Uranus 8:04

This sextile brings unique ideas that help you think outside the box to obtain innovative solutions. Uranus places the focus on rebellion, liberation, and freedom. It adds a dash of spontaneity to your life by bringing a lovely boost of lighter energy that encourages well-being and happiness. It offers food for thought as you get busy sharing with companions. It opens a path that liberates your mood with an influx of options to explore.

30 Sunday

The changes ahead bring intelligent and connected energy into your social life. It promotes growth, expansion, and social involvement. A wellspring of possibilities nurtures heightened social abilities that see you get involved in a group environment. Invitations flow and usher in exciting options. Cultivating these opportunities to network and mingle draws a pleasing result for your life.

May

Sun	Mon	Tue	Wed	Thu	Fri	Sat
	1	2	3	4	5	6
7	8	9	10	11	12	13
14	15	16	17	18	19	20
21	22	23	24	25	26	27
28	29	30	31			

AQUARIUS VIRGO TAURUS SCORPIO MARS STARS SUN WEDDING WEALTH FORTUNE ARIES CAPRICORN CALENDAR GEMINI LOVE ASTROLOGY MOON MONTH LEO HOROSCOPE SAGITTARIUS HAPPINESS BIRTHDAY ASTRONOMY CANCER LIBRA NEPTUNE DATE ZODIAC EARTH SIGN PISCES SKY TODAY DAILY WEEKLY CONSTELLATION MONTHLY

New Moon

Flower Moon

May

1 Monday ~ Beltane/May Day, Pluto turns retrograde in Aquarius 18:39, Sun conjunct Mercury 23:27

Pluto is the modern ruler of Scorpio; it symbolizes how we experience power, renewal, rebirth, and mysterious or subconscious forces. This retrograde phase lasts until October. It allows you to dive deep and explore inner realms and darker aspects of your personality ordinarily hidden from view. Understanding your psyche deeper provides access to the forces driving your personality. It lets you comprehend the why and wherefore behind desires.

2 Tuesday

The wheels are in motion to bring options that improve your life's possibilities. It puts your foot on the accelerator as you get the green light to merge inspiration with creativity and growth. Setting your mind to developing goals helps you chart a course towards a lofty vision that feels meant for your life. It brings a time of advancing skills and refining your abilities as you get a leg up to a new area.

3 Wednesday

Your career path heads towards an upswing. New information currently circulating in the background emerges to offer advancement. It brings a venture worth developing, bringing valuable results that light the way forward. Ideas and creativity are peaking during this vital time of building skills and forging a path toward long-term dreams. It attracts leads that ramp up the potential in your working life.

4 Thursday ~ Venus square Neptune 17:40

A Venus square Neptune aspect offers a dreamy quality. It provides the perfect vibe for engaging in the big sky and dreaming about your perfect romantic escapade. While fairytales in the sky offer relaxation and escapism, it's important to remember that this dreaminess could lead to delusion if you overly focus on something out of reach. Understanding the escapism and creative elements at play enables you to dream big and still feel grounded in reality.

MAY

5 Friday ~ Venus sextile Jupiter 4:02, Flower Full Moon in Scorpio 17:34 Penumbral Lunar Eclipse

The Venus and Jupiter sextile create beneficial and harmonious vibrations for your romantic life. Good luck, and rising prospects bring warmth and social engagement. You connect with kindred spirits and enjoy some well-earned downtime. Replenishing your emotional tanks stabilizes foundations and opens the page to a new chapter. It shines a potent light on personal goals.

6 Saturday ~ Eta Aquarids Meteor Shower April 19th - May 28th

A social environment ahead promotes an uptick of potential for your life. It brings sunshine after rain as it points you towards a happy journey that leaves past struggles behind in the wake of your new life. A carefree chapter brings a spring to your step as you discover a journey that tempts you forward. Magic and romance beckon your life, bringing companionship to the forefront of your world.

7 Sunday ~ Venus ingress Cancer 14:20

Venus brings a sunny aspect that opens to an upward trend ahead. An engaging environment connects with lively discussions, thoughts, and ideas planted for future growth. It all helps build a path forward as you invest time and energy in nurturing stable foundations in your life. Changes in your broader social environment help leave behind issues and drama. It brings an exciting chapter of lively discussions and thoughtful dialogues.

May

8 Monday

Advancement ahead takes you towards a transition that helps you plot a course towards developing your skills. It ushers in growth and learning, increasing wisdom. Exploring leads ignites inspiration and enables you to reach for something more in your working life. You enter an extended time of developing career goals that advance your situation forward. Progression is the logical result of the work you undertake.

9 Tuesday ~ Sun conjunct Uranus 19:55

It is a time of change that helps you create a breakthrough. New possibilities emerge which keep you busy and active with developing working goals. Refining your skills heightens security and creates space to learn in an area that grabs your attention. It opens up a journey that enables you to establish your talents in an exciting direction. It brings a time that highlights more stability flowing in as you launch towards growth in the career sector.

10 Wednesday

Being methodical and paying attention to detail enables you to score a significant victory. It offers advancement that lets you extend your reach into an exciting area. A lively atmosphere at the crux of this journey generates growth and rising prospects. Evaluating the path ahead heightens the potential around your life. It sets intentions that build a stable way forward.

11 Thursday

Exploring new options for your life opens a path of growth that hits a high note. It brings a transition towards an exciting journey. As you draw new possibilities into your life, it harnesses the essence of manifestation to find the correct route forward. You soon find things take shape in a new and stable landscape. Your willingness to be open to changing things up draws a pleasing result for your life.

May

12 Friday ~ Mercury sextile Saturn 8:32, Last Quarter Moon in Aquarius 14:28

Mercury sextile Saturn boosts your Friday, which helps you tidy up loose ends before the weekend. Mental acuity rises, bringing a focused mind, and increased powers of observation lets you see what needs addressing. Today's other cognitive improvements include excellent concentration, memory, and organization skills. With everything running smoothly in your working life, you can enjoy the weekend ahead, knowing you have taken care of your business.

13 Saturday ~ Mercury sextile Venus 2:41, Venus trine Saturn 6:56

Mercury sextile Venus offers a social and friendly influence making this a great day to connect with your tribe. A fantastic time of abundance and magic reinvents the potential possible in your social life. Surprise communication arrives out of the left field. It fuels an exciting chapter of sharing thoughtful dialogues and insightful conversations. It brings liberation, freedom, and expansion into your social life. It is trusting instincts that guide you correctly.

14 Sunday ~ Mother's Day (US)

Developing your life around the home nurtures a balanced and stable environment. It brings ample time to connect with friends, and improving your circumstances is a significant part of this process. An optimistic outlook places you in alignment to expand your horizons. An invitation ahead hits a sweet note in your social life, bringing a whirlwind of activity that promotes excitement into your world.

May

15 Monday ~ Mercury turns direct in Taurus 3:16, Mars trine Neptune 13:44

With Mercury turning direct today, the focus is on your social life. Mars forms a trine with Neptune, enhancing potential as confidence rises and you feel ready for social engagement. It offers the perfect solution for the dodgems as you get busy being self-expressive, communicative, and creative. It opens the door to a fresh start, paving the way toward a more connected environment. Thoughtful discussions and insightful conversations stir the pot of manifestation.

16 Tuesday ~ Jupiter ingress Taurus 17:01

Setting aspirations is a decisive step forward that helps you explore new opportunities. A theme of abundance, security, and renewal supports your growth and evolution. Being proactive lets you discover a journey that speaks to your heart. It unfurls new possibilities that spring to life, a glorious chapter that nurtures creativity and balances foundations. Good fortune flows in and finds its level of happiness and harmony.

17 Wednesday

Unexpected news ahead brings an open road of possibility into your life. It opens the path towards increasing luck and optimism. It lets you make strides in developing an area that becomes an immersive pet project. The future ripples with inspiration as you deepen your knowledge and cultivate advancement. Working with your abilities attracts an engaging and happy journey.

18 Thursday ~ Jupiter square Pluto 1:09, Sun sextile Neptune 8:59

Today's Jupiter square Pluto brings extra drive and increased energy to complete projects and finish your to-do list. Neptune also boosts your goals as a sextile with the Sun helps you find the resources and support needed to manifest your vision. You can bring your dreams to reality as the planets have your back today, attracting rising prospects into your life. Stabilizing foundations lets you make headway towards improving circumstances.

MAY

19 Friday ~ Mercury sextile Saturn 6:50 New Moon in Taurus 15:54

Today, Mercury, Saturn sextile boosts your communication skills and confidence. Add in a dash of New Moon inspiration and aspiration, and you have the perfect mix for engaging in brainstorming with valued companions. Sharing ideas and adding creative ingredients into the pot of manifestation helps you develop a winning trajectory to grow your world. Getting involved with a unique and lively area offers a vibrant time to cultivate your abilities.

20 Saturday ~ Mars ingress Leo 15:24

Mars lands in Leo, and this raises confidence. It's time to go big and be proud and bold. Change is in the air, and exploring a community setting with friends and companions nurtures well-being and harmony. It brings ideas and options that grow your world outwardly. It promotes being adaptive, adventurous, and creative. A purposeful push towards developing your goals brings a pleasing result to light.

21 Sunday ~ Mars opposed Pluto 3:11, Sun ingress Gemini 7:04, Sun trine Pluto 13:58

Mars connects with a competitive edge today that could see your authority tested. The Sun trine Pluto aspect also fuels the fire, increasing your desire to gain power and feed your ambitious streak. You seek opportunities to elevate your standing among peers and co-workers today. Climbing the ladder towards success becomes a dominant factor.

MAY

22 Monday ~ Victoria Day (Canada), Sun sextile Mars 5:56

The Sun sextile Mars transit brings vital energy and renewed zest for life. Upcoming changes leave you feeling enthusiastic about life. It triggers a social aspect that offers new friendships in an expansive and lively environment. New possibilities emerge as a source of inspiration; it reminds you of your passion for life as it reconnects you with an energetic flow of creativity. Sharing with a tribe of like-minded people who support your work cultivates well-being.

23 Tuesday ~ Mars square Jupiter 5:13

Today's Mars square Jupiter offers a positive influence that increases stamina and boosts your energy. Enthusiasm for the task at hand rises, boosting productivity and enabling you to deal with the day's demands efficiently and capably. It is a busy time that keeps you on your toes as an influx of news and information draws opportunities for your life. This enterprising activity brings a lighter flow of energy into your life which lifts flagging spirits.

24 Wednesday

Listening to your instincts sees life take a turn for the better as your social life blossom and grows. You discover new assignments and projects that keep your creatively humming along. It enables you to establish a balanced and grounded foundation and take advantage of curious new prospects that bubble up to keep life exciting.

25 Thursday ~ Shavuot (Begins at sunset)

You will have an opportunity to develop an area that offers improvement. Working on your goals will see an influx of favorable signs that let you know you can create progress if you focus on achieving your best. Planning and tweaking projects will offer rising results that bring valuable rewards flowing into your life. Your willingness to be adaptable and pivot at a moment's notice will come in handy when surprise news lands in your lap.

MAY

26 Friday ~ Venus sextile Uranus 7:36

Today's sextile promotes a vibrant and active social life. With Venus charming and Uranus adding a dash of spontaneity to your weekend plans, it assures a fun and lively time shared with friends. Reawakening to the potential that seeks to tempt you forward empowers your spirit. It sees you becoming more involved in expanding your social life. Spending time with friends is rocket fuel for your creativity as it brings new ideas to contemplate.

27 Saturday ~ Shavuot (Ends at sunset), First Quarter Moon in Virgo 15:22

Life becomes more socially connected and enriching as you expand your horizons and link up with others with similar interests. It offers notable changes that highlight a journey that develops your social life. It promotes a busy and lively time of social inclusion as you mingle with friends who nurture happiness. Constructive dialogues bring news and insight into areas worth developing.

28 Sunday

Life brims with unique potential. Exploring a variety of interests and pathways reawakens your sense of adventure. You land in an enriching landscape that nurtures creativity and places the spotlight on developing your dreams. Entertaining discussions offer a lively and engaging landscape that encourages happiness and well-being in your life. An emphasis on home life cultivates stable foundations.

June

Sun	Mon	Tue	Wed	Thu	Fri	Sat
				1	2	3
4	5	6	7	8	9	10
11	12	13	14	15	16	17
18	19	20	21	22	23	24
25	26	27	28	29	30	

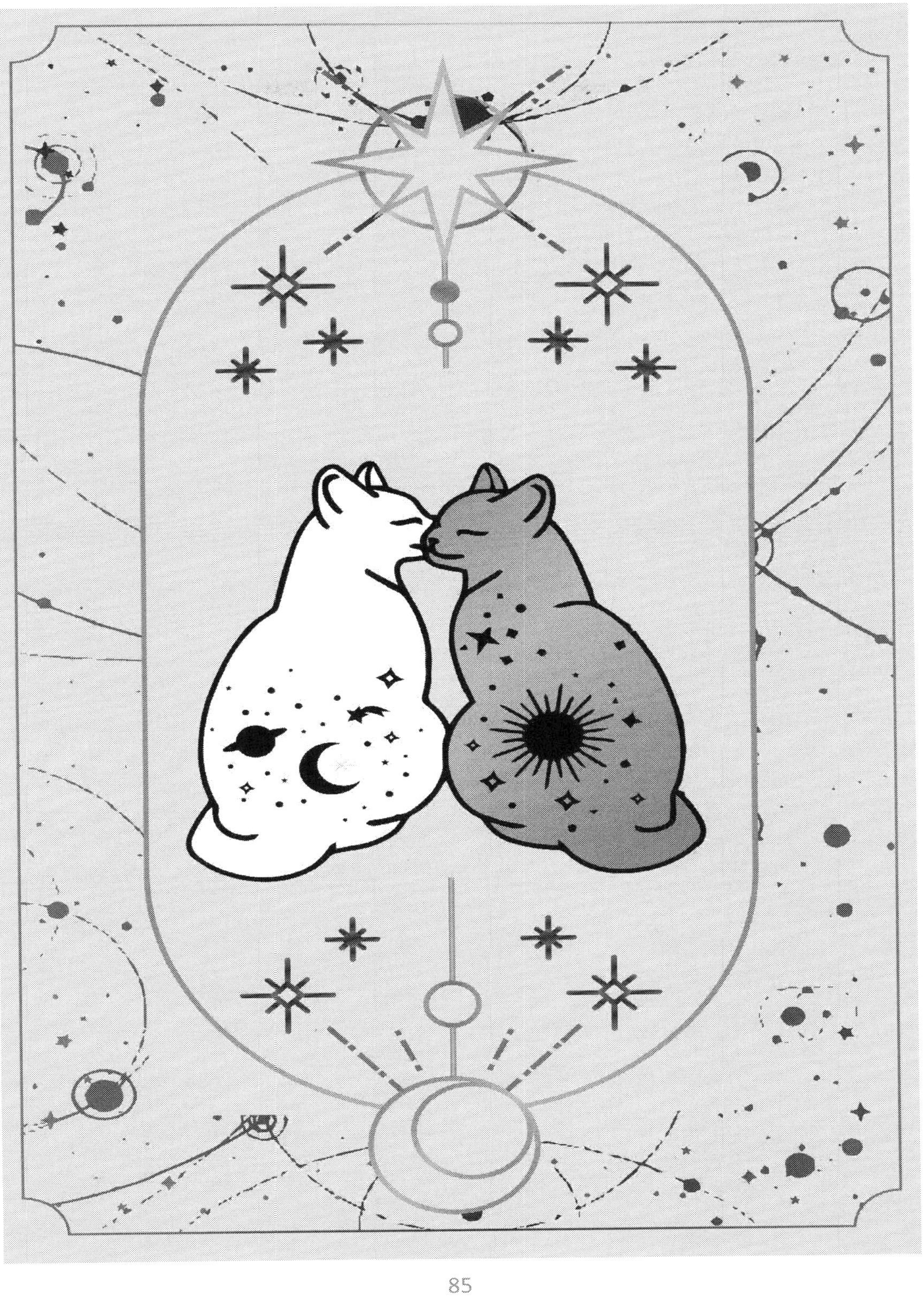

New Moon

Strawberry Moon

MAY/JUNE

29 Monday ~ Memorial Day, Mercury at Greatest Elongation 24.9W

A more social aspect draws liveliness and engagement shared with friends. You attend a gathering with lights, music, and dancing being a feature attraction. It nurtures pathways of romance and connection that lets you face the future with an optimistic approach. Sharing with valued friends brings a busy time filled with promise. It offers an enriching environment that could lead to collaborations by sharing lively discussions and brainstorming with friends.

30 Tuesday

A new role is on offer for your working life. It creates space to advance your talents and establish your skills in a unique area. It brings opportunities to learn and refine your abilities. It opens the door to a journey of growth and evolution that promotes advancement in your career. It leads to a productive and enterprising time that offers growth and prosperity. It does bring new possibilities that link you to positive change.

31 Wednesday

An adventure is looming. It helps you move away from a difficult chapter in your life and head towards an expressive and trailblazing journey. It also connects you with others who understand and support your life. It's a progressive phase that cultivates rising abundance, security, and good fortune. It expands what is possible as it brings an assignment that fosters growth. Doing research and proactively developing the way lets you immerse in new options.

1 Thursday

You are heading into a new growth cycle that supports growing your abilities. You have unique talents that are ready to be developed. Exploring leads helps you sort through the options available in your life. Laying the groundwork brings a balanced foundation from which to grow. Several crosscurrents are flowing through your life, and things become clearer soon. It gives you a clear direction from which to develop your goals.

June

2 Friday ~ Venus trine Neptune 22:42

Creativity and imagination are peaking under the blissful Venus, Neptune trine. Harmony, equilibrium, and well-being soar under this positive influence. Self-expression is rising, cultivating a unique path that captures the essence of artistic inclinations. Venus showers positivity over your social life, improving personal bonds. Curiosity leads to an uplifting time discussing future projects and endeavors with kindred spirits who understands your outlook on life.

3 Saturday

A message arrives for you and activates a fascinating journey that brings new people into your life. Expanding your circle of friends directs your purpose towards improving life. You reveal information that brings a stir of excitement as it opens a gateway forward. You can build a bridge towards a brighter chapter; being open to change lets you see your life with fresh eyes and an open heart.

4 Sunday ~ Strawberry Full Moon in Sagittarius 3:42, Mercury conjunct Uranus 19:50

Mercury and Uranus form a positive aspect that heightens mental abilities. Increasing mental stimulation promotes fresh ideas in your life today. Technology, messages, and communication all spark inspiration and foster possibilities for future development. It allows you to set sail towards a happy chapter that emphasizes improving the foundations of your life.

JUNE

5 Monday ~ Venus ingress Leo 13:42, Venus opposed Pluto 16:04

You may be feeling unsettled and restless. This edgy Venus vibe is a sign to look for new leads, as gaining insight into the path ahead will provide you with a valuable gateway. It is to your benefit to generate new leads and advance your skills. Against what has been an unsettling backdrop, you soon expand your life and move towards developing a new endeavor. Your limitless imagination enables new ideas to spring to life.

6 Tuesday

Information arrives that helps you turn a corner and head towards growth. New demands in your life are coming, but these responsibilities heighten the security in your world. It brings a path that advances your circumstances. You develop an assignment that grows skills and brings expansion to the forefront. Rising prospects let you pour your energy into a venture that enriches and inspires. A unique option emerges that gives you a chance to grow your career path.

7 Wednesday

You may feel restless and ready for the next leg of your journey. New horizons loom overhead and spark a chapter of movement and discovery. It brings options and opportunities which propel life forward toward new adventures. A unique area calls your name, and you get busy establishing grounded foundations that foster a favorable shift ahead. A conscious effort to improve circumstances enables you to progress in life towards advancing a vital goal.

8 Thursday

Unexpected news arrives out of the blue, but it heads your life towards an upswing as new possibilities attract a lighter flow of energy. It lets you chart a course to share an enriching time with friends and companions. It opens the gateway to a dynamic environment that offers trailblazing conversations and thoughtful ideas. It places you on a mission to evolve your talents and nurture your abilities. An emphasis on improving skills promotes advancement.

JUNE

9 Friday

Socializing with your friends delivers a wellspring of opportunities emphasizing a supportive vibe. It helps you build stable foundations that feel comfortable and calming. You connect with friends and companions and relish spending time cultivating social bonds that count. As you become involved with rising potential around your social life, it charts a course towards life-affirming endeavors that renew and rejuvenate your spirit.

10 Saturday ~ Last Quarter Moon in Pisces 19:31

You discover valuable information that opens a pathway towards a lighter chapter. It brings a positive influence into your life which lifts flagging spirits. It kickstarts growth and progress for your social life, and this gets a chance to network with people who offer enriching ideas and insight. Life heads to an upward trend of increasing opportunities to mingle and invitations to connect with friends.

11 Sunday ~ Mercury ingress Gemini 10:24, Mercury trine Pluto 10:27, Pluto ingress Capricorn 13:12, Venus square Jupiter 15:39

Today's Venus square Jupiter planetary alignment offers good things for your social life. It is the perfect time to engage with friends; lively discussions nurture creativity. It is a prime time for letting your hair down and having fun in a relaxing environment that draws stability into your world. It allows you to mingle and network with your broader circle of friends.

JUNE

12 Monday

Refining your abilities draws advancement. It lets you take on an enterprising area that offers rising prospects. You soon build stable foundations which heighten the security around your life. These new options become a catalyst for growth which helps you climb the rungs to a successful outcome. A curious assignment comes calling and lights up development, learning, and prosperity areas.

13 Tuesday

You discover a happy path forward with news that arrives with fresh possibilities. A change of perspective cracks the code as you highlight the information necessary to advance or life into a new area. Optimism and inspiration run wild as you embark on developing unique goals. Channeling your creativity into an enterprising area is the right direction to see life blossom. Growth, advancement, and progress are soon within reach.

14 Wednesday ~ Flag Day

Increasing activity in your social life brings unexpected invitations to mingle. You discover thoughtful discussions are possible with a great mix of people who nurture companionship. Expanding your circle of friends brings good luck into your life. It opens a portal toward social engagement that supports well-being in your world. It attracts an upbeat time of lively discussions. A stable basis for growing your life lets you expand your horizons in a favorable direction.

15 Thursday

The conditions for growth ripen, and you achieve more stability and progression. Well-crafted ideas get a chance to shine. It underscores the essence of manifestation and magic that help you create remarkable progress. You gain traction on developing your vision and enter a cycle of increasing possibility. It helps you set sail on a timely voyage that offers ample room to reinvent your skills in an industry that feels the right fit for your talents.

JUNE

16 Friday

Noticeable changes ahead attract happiness and abundance into your life. It puts you in the proper alignment to grow your circle of friends. An emphasis on expansion brings a breakthrough that hits the ticket for a productive time shared with like-minded people you value. Constructive dialogues provide a thoughtful perspective that brings new ideas and concepts to explore. It brings a creative viewpoint that has you thinking about launching a new area.

17 Saturday ~ Saturn turns Retrograde in Pisces 16:52

Saturn is a planet that rules boundaries, structure, and discipline. This retrograde draws balance and righteousness into your situation. Making fair and reasonable choices and decisions connects with karma to achieve a fair and beneficial outcome. Honesty, integrity, and impartial judgment are essential in making the right choices for your life. You may be about to face a decision in your life.

18 Sunday ~ New Moon in Cancer 4:38, Father's Day (US)

Rejuvenation is a powerful theme that reverberates around your life. It brings a cycle of growth and opportunity that helps you grow your life in a new direction. The energy of manifestation attracts new possibilities that help you turn a corner and head towards a winning chapter. Life blossoms and its pace and becomes more active and social. It sows the seeds for an abundant chapter of sharing quality time with kindred spirits.

June

19 Monday ~ Sun square Neptune 3:53, Jupiter sextile Saturn 15:53

Today, the Neptune square Sun aspect can water down your ambitions, leaving you feeling foggy and indecisive. If your vision feels clouded, going back over your plans can help make sure they continue to align with your vision for future growth. Recommitting to develop your career goals can help shift some of the clouds that hang over your working life today. If the boss gives you a hard time, blame it on Neptune for bringing Monday woes into your working life.

20 Tuesday

Life supports your efforts to improve circumstances. New possibilities spark a journey that offers expansion. It shines a light on goals, status, and career success. Putting the finishing touches on your strategy lets you develop a winning trajectory when news arrives that encourages expansion. Rising prospects open up an avenue that offers growth and security. It allows you to move towards advancement.

21 Wednesday ~ Midsummer/Litha Solstice 14:58, Mercury sextile Mars 15:23

The Mercury sextile Mars aspect today fosters joint projects and cooperation. Getting involved with a group endeavor stimulates your mind and brings new possibilities. Brainstorming sessions offer a trailblazing path towards innovative solutions and rising prospects. Joining forces and strategizing with like-minded people cultivate an excellent success rate. It helps you cover the bases by blending other people's talents into the mix of potential at your disposal.

22 Thursday

Changes ahead keep you on your toes. It brings a positive aspect that revolutionizes the potential possible in your world. Surging optimism brings pep to your step. Marching to the beat of your drum, you make inroads into growing a creative enterprise that nurtures your talents. Dabbling in areas that spark your attention promotes well-being and stabilizes foundations. It brings a chance to share your gifts with an audience, which feels like a bold move towards success.

JUNE

23 Friday

Much potential takes you towards a phase of expansion, prosperity, and growth. It has you working on larger goals. It brings a venture that captures your interest. This area allows you to develop an endeavor that inspires your mind. It is a good time when you take steps toward progressing your goals. There is plenty to celebrate ahead; gathering friends brings lively discussions. It paves the way toward growth and rejuvenation.

24 Saturday

A new start flows into your life; it shines a light on a productive time that creates a strong basis for developing new goals and dreams. Creativity leads the way forward towards a vital shift that offers expansion in your social life. It connects you with kindred spirits who nurture an abundant landscape. Sharing your ideas with a tribe of creative people promotes a supportive environment. An area you encourage blossoms and draw ample time for soul-stirring conversations.

25 Sunday

A blank canvas of new options tempts you to develop your creativity in a unique area. It opens a path that grows your world and improves the foundations of your life. Effectively channeling your energy into creating your dreams brings a turning point that offers room to advance your talents. It brings a journey that is inspiring, thought-provoking, and trailblazing. The atmosphere of abundance draws rising confidence which attracts new friends and companions.

JUNE

26 Monday ~ First Quarter Moon in Libra 7:50, Mars square Uranus 9:22

You soon chart a course towards a brighter chapter and enter a growth-orientated time that brings a productive landscape into view. As you head into this time of opportunity, it takes your life towards unique areas that grow your talents. It deepens knowledge and refines skills, giving you the green light to grow your career path. Rising prospects attract advancement to your career.

27 Tuesday ~ Mercury ingress Cancer 12:22

Evaluating options takes you towards a new chapter that has you feeling excited about the possibilities in your life. Planning and developing future goals lets you stake your claim on improving your life as it gives you the green light to make yourself a priority. An emphasis on enhancing your circumstances attracts a valuable result. It transitions you to new options that encourage growth and learning.

28 Wednesday

Opportunities to improve your working life draw stability and growth. Rising prospects open up new leads to refine your skills and talents. Nurturing your abilities draws an abundant landscape that enables you to gain traction on advancing life forward. It seals the lid on a problematic chapter that feels finished. You get busy and embark on growing your world in a unique and inspiring direction.

29 Thursday ~ Sun trine Saturn 1:42

Today's Sun trine Saturn offers constructive dialogues and thoughtful ideas that enhance your creativity and stimulate new pathways of possibility in your life. A positive influence nurtures unique approaches that capitalize on the potential possible in your surroundings. It brings thoughtful discussions that offer support and news. It enables you to embrace a journey that nurtures well-being and harmony.

July

Sun	Mon	Tue	Wed	Thu	Fri	Sat
						1
2	3	4	5	6	7	8
9	10	11	12	13	14	15
16	17	18	19	20	21	22
23	24	25	26	27	28	29
30	31					

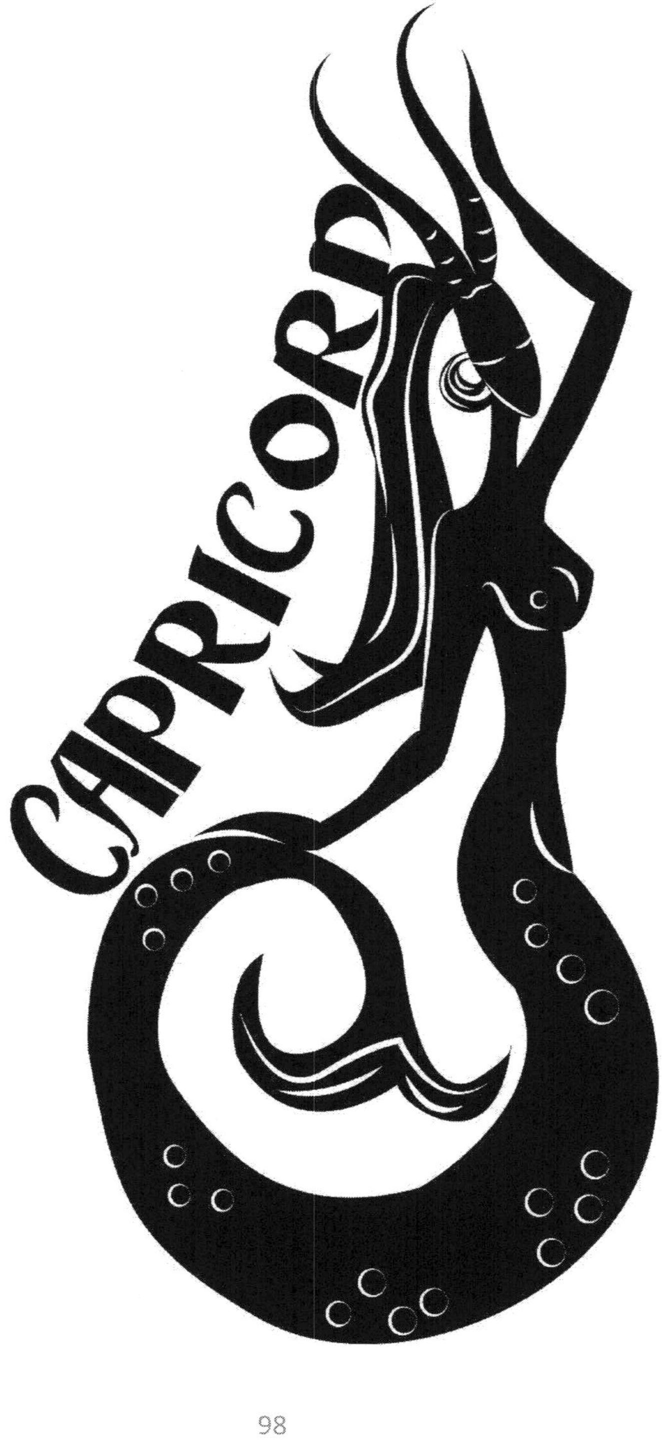
CAPRICORN

New Moon

Buck Moon

June/July

30 Friday ~ Neptune turns Retrograde in Pisces, 19:28

Neptune retrograde strips away delusions, allusions, and fanciful thinking. Under the glare of more informed thought processes, you build tangible growth pathways to take your talents to the next level. This phase lets you sink your teeth into developing goals that offer fruitful results. Moving away from areas that have clouded your thinking and brought doubt to your judgment does provide you with clear stepping stones that take you towards success.

1 Saturday ~ Canada Day, Sun conjunct Mercury 5:05, Mercury sextile Jupiter 7:10, Sun sextile Jupiter 10:26

Open-mindedness, curiosity, and a quest for adventure are prominent aspects as a Mercury sextile Jupiter alignment fosters creativity and self-expression. This transit favors organization, planning, and the development of longer-term goals. Reviewing plans and streamlining your vision enables you to cut to the chase and find a practical path to progress your goals. New information emerges to catch your interest and spur you to advance your life.

2 Sunday ~ Venus square Uranus 14:32

An increased need for freedom and liberation can destabilize as Venus faces Uranus in a square alignment. Being mindful of balancing interpersonal bonds while being self-expressive and creative can ease tensions. At the same time, you can let your hair down and enjoy a freedom-driven chapter of fun and excitement. Being open to new people and possibilities helps you rise above troubles and embrace an enriching social time.

JULY

3 Monday ~ Super Moon, Buck Full Moon in Capricorn 11:40

It marks a time of rejuvenation that smooths over the rough edges. Sweeping away areas no longer relevant lets you shift your focus towards expansively developing your life. Curious changes ahead bring a fresh cycle of growth into your life. You soon discover an engaging environment that lifts the lid on a beautiful journey forward for your world. It brings an emphasis on developing companionship.

4 Tuesday ~ Independence Day

You embark on a chapter that focuses on developing key areas of your life. It lets you forge ahead and embrace a lovely time of expanding horizons. Your situation is evolving, bringing new possibilities into your life. Sifting and sorting through options lets you unearth a suitable opportunity to nurture. It brings a time of change and excitement as you set sail on a voyage that captures the essence of adventure.

5 Wednesday

Thinking hard about future possibilities brings a dream into focus. Setting intentions helps you become confident about chasing your vision and developing lofty goals. Opportunities arrive that offer progression and advancement. It promotes a journey of growth and refinement. Working with your abilities enables you to channel your skills and effectively create change productively.

6 Thursday

You enter a vital time for being productive, which enhances project development. Life hums along as you immerse yourself in growing your life. It launches a time that offers to deepen your knowledge and refine your skills. Working on assignments draws a good pace that enables you to achieve positive results. Information arrives that cracks the code to grow your abilities in a new area.

July

7 Friday

An opportunity is coming up for you that will be a good fit for your life. As you step out on a journey of increasing possibilities, life becomes lighter and sweeter. A creative venture becomes a hot topic of conversation in your circle of friends. It activates a group environment that nurtures your talents as you contribute knowledge and share your skills with others. It brings an enterprising time that keeps you on your toes.

8 Saturday

Life leads to a fantastic time that expands the boundaries of your life. It gives room to cultivate a new interest and dabble in hobbies that promote well-being and happiness. Many raw potentials are ready to connect you with a circle of like-minded individuals. It illustrates what you can achieve by staying open to change and exploring the broader world of potential outside your door. Lightness and momentum carry you forward.

9 Sunday ~ Mercury trine Neptune 23:56

Mercury in trine with Neptune focuses on your dreams and goals; it adds mental clarity that helps you stay focused as you work towards realizing your vision. Something you hope to reach in your life can reach fruition with the correct planning, adjustments, and focus. Creating space to nurture your priorities lets you reap the rewards of a dedicated approach that offers an increasing success rate.

July

10 Monday ~ Last Quarter Moon in Aries 1:48, Mars ingress Virgo 11:34, Mercury opposed Pluto 20:47

As you launch plans to improve your circumstances, you enter a productive time working with your abilities to grow your skills. Beginning a new project can feel overwhelming, but breaking your goals into smaller sections helps keep things manageable. Tracking progress enables motivation to keep humming along as you get busy charting a course towards your vision.

11 Tuesday ~ Mercury ingress Leo 4:09

An experimental flavor draws a new influence into your life. Reshuffling the decks of potential opens a curious path forward. It brings an emphasis on growing unique dreams and goals that offer expansion. Developments let the puzzle pieces fall into place, creating a beautiful picture of what is possible when you believe in yourself. It leaves you feeling optimistic about the future.

12 Wednesday

You have lots happening on the schedule soon. Advancement results from your quest as an emphasis on improving your life open opportunities to help you move upwards and achieve greatness. Working towards your vision for the future draws a pleasing result. A positive influence raises confidence and enables you to build a concrete path forward. Taking advantage of all the options ahead rekindles vitality.

13 Thursday

Information arrives that enables you to head towards a winning streak in your life. It offers a journey that attracts new pathways. Seeing what is possible when you expand your horizons draws inspiration, encouraging you to keep moving toward your goals. Investing in your life shapes your world and aligns it with the person you are becoming; developing hopes and dreams ushers in a pleasing result.

JULY

14 Friday ~ Sun sextile Uranus 23:02

In sextile with the Sun, Uranus captures the essence of surprises, new information, and discoveries. Something new and exciting is ready to manifest in your life. Catching up with friends nurtures well-being and places you in the correct alignment to grow your social life. Being open to new people and possibilities charts a course towards rising prospects. It leads to more social engagement, and focusing on sharing with others gets valuable results.

15 Saturday

You enter a soul-stirring time that lifts the lid on growth in your romantic life. It kicks off a journey of sunshine, sparkle, and romance. Lighting up pathways of increasing connection and emotional harmony brings an active time of developing romance in your life. Riding a wave of inspiration carries you along when nurturing your dreams. It does place you in alignment to grow a meaningful path forward for your love life.

16 Sunday

You enter a time of metamorphosis that removes outworn layers. Peeling back the possibilities takes you to a significant chapter that charts a course towards developing unique options in your life. It opens the floodgates to rising prospects that bring vibrancy and renewal. An optimistic and abundant mindset promotes advancement. You enter a busy time that brings growth and expansion your way.

July

17 Monday ~ Mercury square Jupiter 12:48, New Moon in Cancer 18:32

You can reach for the gold at the rainbow's end. Chasing dreams brings advancement and inspiration into your world. It offers a chance to improve circumstances as you unearth a discovery that becomes a jewel in your crown. It lets you progress and expand horizons into new areas as you develop a project right for progression. Being open to new possibilities helps you thrive during uncertain times.

18 Tuesday ~ Islamic New Year

Good news arrives with a flurry. It brings an essential clue into the journey which awaits your open energy and curious mind. Greener pastures beckon as you launch life forward and head towards growth. Indeed, new possibilities raise confidence and are a source of inspiration in your world. It ignites a passion for life that revitalizes and rekindles your spirit.

19 Wednesday

As you gain traction on advancing life forward, you discover an enterprising journey that offers progress. Serendipity lights the way ahead, bringing new possibilities into your life. Change is coming; staying open to growing your life attracts an upward trend as you discover an avenue to revolutionize the path ahead. Channeling your energy into nurturing your dreams brings a comprehensive approach that provides a pleasing result.

20 Thursday ~ Sun trine Neptune 13:06, Mars opposed Saturn 20:39

The Sun trine Neptune alignment raises the vibration around your life. It focuses on improving the circumstances in your life and helping others who face difficult circumstances. Creativity is a valuable resource that lets you craft plans that offer tangible impacts that enhance your world. Curiosity leads you towards a little worn path that offers growth and refinement of talents. Getting involved with working with your abilities draws a pleasing result.

JULY

21 Friday

The borders of your world open and draw a refreshing time shared with friends. You unlock a vibrant atmosphere that grows your world in a supportive direction. Sharing time with friends rejuvenates your energy and restores equilibrium. It offers grounded foundations that promote balance and harmony. You get in touch with a lighter, more playful side of life as fun and friendship take prominence.

22 Saturday ~ Sun opposed Pluto 3:52

The Sun shines a light on a hidden aspect Pluto keeps out of sight in your day-to-day life. This opposition Pluto creates a doorway through which pockets of the inner self, spirit, and primal energy can reach the surface of your awareness. It shines a light on subconscious desires and instincts. Life has an edgier aspect that can feel unsettling today. It does get you in touch with hidden depths that spark an internal dialogue as you reveal a personal element of your personality.

23 Sunday ~ Venus turns Retrograde in Leo 1:33, Sun ingress Leo 1:47

Venus turns retrograde, which slows the progress down around your love life. Romantic development slows down or stagnates during this phase. Focus on the building blocks as the journey is as important as the final destination. As progress slows, you may feel more sensitive and lack insight into the path ahead. Understanding that Venus is working in the background to solidify foundations enables you to focus on the building blocks of your life.

JULY

24 Monday

As you create a bridge towards growing your dreams, you discover a venture that opens the door wide. A turning point occurs that offers advancement for your working life. It lets you dive into uncharted territory and find growth is possible when you push against the barriers of perceived expectations. An opportunity ahead fosters rising optimism. You get involved in learning an area that holds water and revs up the success rate for your career.

25 Tuesday ~ First Quarter Moon in Libra 22:06

Formulating a plan brings improvement as you map out a trajectory that offers a stellar degree of growth. You generate luck and expansion by your willingness to work on your life. Focusing on a pioneering path takes you closer to realizing your dreams. Setting intentions brings key avenues into focus. Planting the seeds for future growth enables life to blossom under sunny skies. It brings a happy time that captures the essence of excitement.

26 Wednesday

As you dig deeper into what motivates and inspires your life, you discover insight into the path ahead. Planning and preparation enable you to plot a course towards developing your aspirations. You find you can break fresh ground and establish your talents in a progressive area worth your time. Designing your life becomes a strong emphasis that opens a journey of new possibilities.

27 Thursday ~ Mercury conjunct Venus 15:15

The Mercury conjunct Venus aspect today bodes well for your personal life. Communication flows, as does feelings, emotions, and sentiments. The time is right to share loving thoughts and receive positive feedback from someone who holds meaning in your life. Speaking your mind and letting your presence be known places the spotlight on growing your world in a romantic direction.

July

28 Friday ~ Delta Aquarids Meteor Shower. July 12th – August 23rd, Mercury ingress Virgo 21:29

You soon crack the code to a bright chapter in your social life. It expands your circle of friends and brings companionship and joint ventures to light. Many hands make light work, and getting involved in a group environment with creative types, lifts the lid on a happy and relaxing atmosphere. Dabbling in innovative enterprises is therapeutic and promotes wellness and harmony.

29 Saturday

A social aspect ahead brings helpful news. Sharing with friends and leaning into a supportive environment nurtures balanced foundations. It creates space to contemplate the path forward in a relaxed and ambient atmosphere. Lighter energy encourages rejuvenation and promotes renewal in your life. This positive influence enables you to re-stabilize any ragged foundations and builds grounded power around your home life.

30 Sunday

A cheerful chapter ahead grows your social life. It shines a light on a stabilizing environment that contributes to rock-solid foundations in your world. From this stable basis, you get involved with group projects and joined forces with others who offer creative insights and ideas into areas worth developing. It lets you sink your teeth into a journey that channels your abilities into growing an exciting enterprise.

August

Sun	Mon	Tue	Wed	Thu	Fri	Sat
		1	2	3	4	5
6	7	8	9	10	11	12
13	14	15	16	17	18	19
20	21	22	23	24	25	26
27	28	29	30	31		

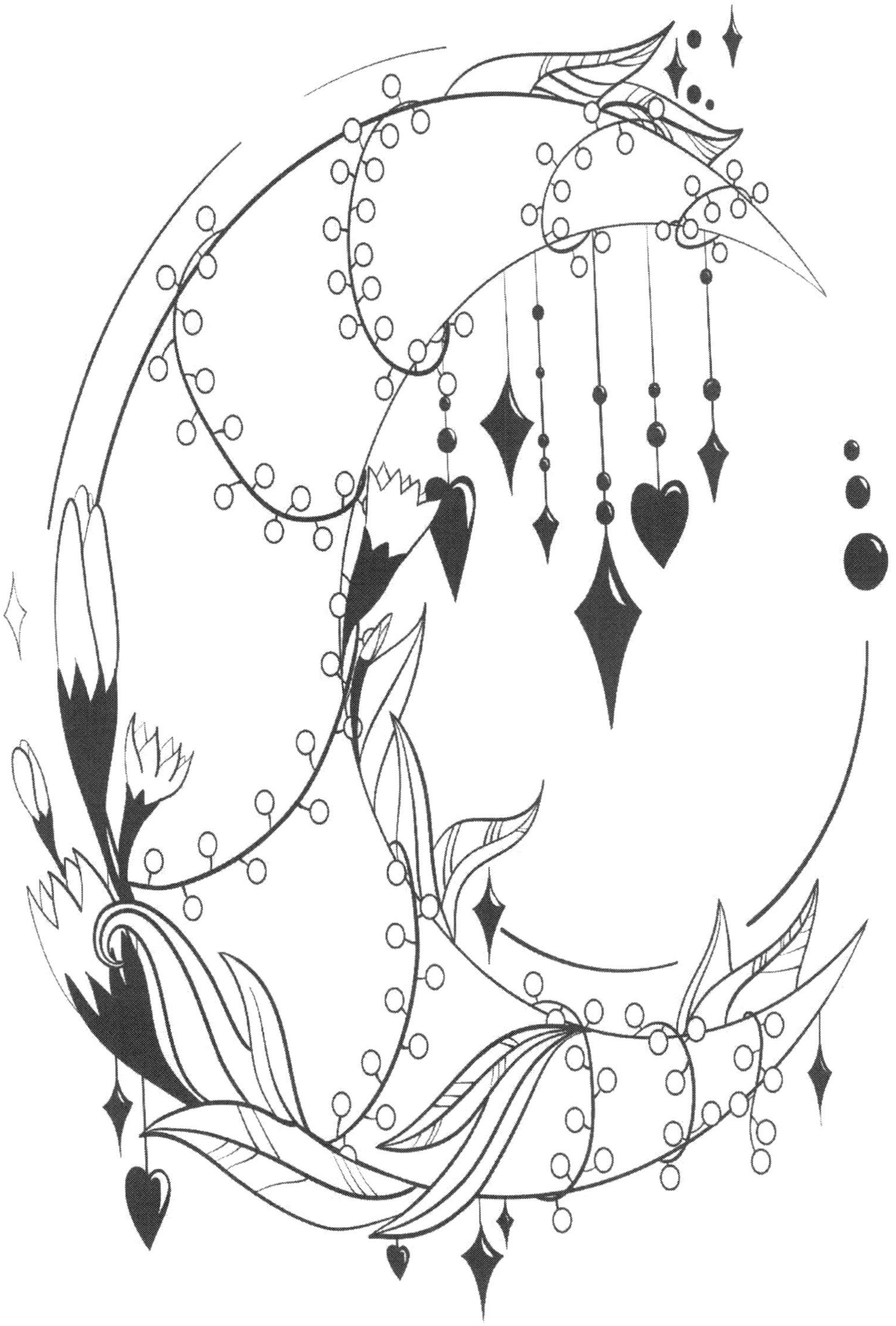

New Moon

Sturgeon Moon

July/August

31 Monday

Being heedless of boundaries and courageously following your enthusiasm helps you build your life from scratch. It brings new options that enable you to dare dream and wonder about future possibilities. Your brilliant mind brings the right idea to develop. Before long, you discover that you are on to something significant that enables you to establish your promising ideas with purpose and capability.

1 Tuesday ~ Lammas/Lughnasadh, Super Moon, Sturgeon Full Moon in Aquarius 18:32, Mars trine Jupiter 20:44

Deep reflection and contemplation are helpful tools to release sensitive areas and restore balance. It does help you prepare the groundwork before you become busy growing your life outwardly. You discover rising prospects, enabling you to enjoy a social aspect that offers engagement and mingling. Sharing thoughtful conversations with friends draws possibilities to your world.

2 Wednesday ~ Mercury opposed Saturn 2:16

As Mercury opposes Saturn, it brings heavy vibes into your life. The air of tension leaves a palpable sense of negativity around conversations and communication today. A serious-minded person may seek to have a strongly worded conversation with you. Setting boundaries and creating space to nurture the foundations in your life helps restore balance if talks become pessimistic today. Pushing business decisions off for another day is advisable.

3 Thursday

News arrives for you soon that fans the flames of inspiration. It attracts rising possibilities that grow your skills as you launch towards developing your dreams. You establish your abilities in a productive and purposeful environment ripe with opportunity. The magic of your creativity stimulates growth and allows you to manifest a pleasing result in your life. It attracts a productive environment with a positive aspect that nurtures craftsmanship.

August

4 Friday

Opening your life to new pathways lets you head toward rising growth and inspiring prospects. Good luck, fans flames of inspiration, as you embark on a monumental shift towards growing your life outwardly. You enjoy a light-hearted journey shared with friends as you broaden your horizons. It sees excellent improvement in friendship, romance, and connection, bringing laughter and liveliness ahead.

5 Saturday

A change ahead helps release past issues that stalled progress around your life. News arrives that delivers exciting possibilities as it offers room to mingle and connect with your social life more often. A mix of manifestations at your disposal helps brew a refreshing time to expand your circle. Mingling with others draws fresh ideas as possibilities bounce around in an engaging atmosphere.

6 Sunday

Positive energy flows into your life, bringing a warm glow to your spirit. It sets the scene to nurture abundance as a positive influence arrives to boost well-being and harmony. You enter a richly enjoyable environment that promotes social ties and friendships. It brings the chance to mingle and share thoughtful discussions that enrich your world. Moving out of your usual routine and circulating with your circle of friends puts the spotlight on a lively environment.

AUGUST

7 Monday ~ Sun square Jupiter 12:03

Today's Sun square Jupiter aspect raises confidence and brings good fortune swirling around your life. It does boost your ego, which could lead to you overstepping the mark. Knowing your capabilities and working within the systems you have in place for your life will help keep things in check during this energetic time. Developments ahead create a solid basis that heads towards advancement.

8 Tuesday ~ Last Quarter Moon in Taurus 10:48

Alchemy is currently brewing in your life's background. You soon open a journey that offers handsome returns on your time. Investing your energy in developing this journey brings the correct path forward for your life. The crux of designing your life in a new journey ahead is a richly creative process. You attract positive results as the essence of manifestation carries you along.

9 Wednesday ~ Venus square Uranus 11:09

A surprise element adds a sense of uncertainty to your personal/social life due to the Venus square Uranus aspect today. You are in a time of transformation, and this can feel unsettling. It promotes a restless vibe that encourages you to head towards expansion. Information that crosses your path opens an avenue worth developing. A helping hand from someone in the background pulls the strings that open the gate to a brighter chapter in your life.

10 Thursday ~ Mercury at Greatest Elongation 27.4 E, Mercury trine Jupiter 12:45

Mercury trine Jupiter today brings a boost to your life. Jupiter is the planet of good luck and fortuitous happenings, which improves the potential possible around your circumstances. It brings a busy time for socializing as a clear path opens and connects you with opportunities to network and mingle. Indeed, this aspect sees life becoming more active and connected. Sharing with friends brings a positive influence on your surroundings.

August

11 Friday

A busy time brings an end to disappointing delays. You get the ball rolling on a social chapter that brings new people to your life. It sparks a supportive journey that offers pearls of wisdom as thoughtful discussions draw unique insight into the path ahead. Nurturing companionship heightens the sense of well-being and harmony. You discover a journey that offers room to learn a new area and soon thrive in a productive environment.

12 Saturday ~ Perseids Meteor Shower July 17th - Aug 24th

Opportunities ahead link up a more social environment for your life. Lively energy percolating in the background makes the dashing entrance into your world. It draws a bountiful time that nurtures entertaining discussions, insight, and news. Sharing with friends takes you towards a chapter that is brighter, lighter, and filled with good intentions. Being receptive to change and flexible brings a spontaneous and lively environment into view.

13 Sunday

As your social life expands, it creates space for new adventures to take flight. It draws abundance and invites joy into your world. Social invitations tempt you out in your broader community. This expansion is a pivotal time where you connect with unique people and possibilities. It delivers warmth, friendship, and advancement. Doors open and head you towards a social environment that stimulates creativity and energizes your spirit.

August

14 Monday

Prepare to embark on growing your life outwardly. Indeed, exciting news arrives, which is a catalyst for change. The timing is fortunate; it is a sign that you can advance your goals and head toward growing your dreams. Rising prospects on the horizon ensure a pleasing result for your life. Let your creativity be your guide on this journey. It gives you a broader reach of what is possible when you spread your wings and take flight towards growing life outwardly.

15 Tuesday

A new journey is ready to begin your life. News arrives, which offers an opportunity for growth. It opens a positive trend that helps you make tracks towards developing an exciting area worth your time. Advancement is imminent, and you can build a pleasing result by being open to new possibilities that cross your path. It is an ideal time to explore nurturing new areas and extend your reach into progressing a curious assignment that comes calling.

16 Wednesday ~ Sun square Uranus 2:34, New Moon in Leo 09:37, Mars trine Uranus 13:53

Uranus steals the show today, and you can expect a spontaneous and expressive environment that offers a breath of fresh air in your life. You head to a chapter that holds great promise. It closes the door on past issues and removes barriers limiting your life progress. It lets you take a leap of faith and embrace developing a curious journey.

17 Thursday

Mapping out a plan helps you plot a course towards a lofty goal. It positions you to open a path that progressively extends your skills. More excellent stability and advancement are the foundation of this journey. You soon reveal an exciting possibility that redefines what you thought was possible. Deepening your talents and working with your abilities will draw pleasing results. It sets the tone for a prosperous path that brings a sweet flavor into your life.

AUGUST

18 Friday

Information arrives that may throw you off balance. Still, it is a catalyst for positive change in your life. It puts you in touch with the liberating sense of freedom that lets you pass the threshold and enter a brighter time of developing opportunities. Getting in touch with forgotten hobbies and talents that have drifted to the wayside will bring inspiring projects to the forefront of your life. You soon notice signs that life is heading towards a chapter without barriers.

19 Saturday

You are ready to attract abundance into your life. Keeping your eyes open for new possibilities helps you reveal a diamond. This opportunity appears to come out of the blue but is a significant path in your life. Serendipity and signs help guide you correctly towards a new endeavor. Progress moves quickly, enabling you to take advantage of developing a passion project. It sweeps away outworn energy and creates space for inspiration to light the path forward.

20 Sunday

Curious events on the horizon draw refreshing possibilities into your life. You open a social chapter that brings a shift forward, leading to a wellspring of abundance. Communication ahead opens lively dialogues with friends as an invitation to mingle hits a high note in your life. It ushers in a journey of change and potential that attracts enriching moments shared with people you value. Hearing from people in your circle brings a warm glow that nurtures well-being.

AUGUST

21 Monday

Taking full advantage of the opportunities ahead brings a productive and full schedule. A flurry of activity has you feeling valued and appreciated. Life brings new assignments and projects that are useful in establishing a grounded and balanced environment. New prospects bubble up to keep your creative energy sparking. Significant changes ahead draw good fortune into your world. You cast your net wide and discover pleasing results.

22 Tuesday ~ Venus square Jupiter 12:13, Mars opposed Neptune 20:33

A Venus Jupiter square offers rising prospects for your love life. You will have trouble concentrating on the task as fun moments capture your attention. It brings a positive influence that improves the happiness in your life. It brings a romantic situation into view that excites you about the possibilities. You receive essential news that enables you to grow your world outwardly and embrace a social aspect that nurtures magic in your life.

23 Wednesday ~ Sun ingress Virgo 8:58, Mercury turns retrograde 19:59

Mercury turns retrograde and puts a damper on the potential possible in your social life. It can cause miscommunication and issues in your love life. Mercury in retrograde adds an element that turns communication haywire. It disrupts the positive flow of energy in your life. Delay signing contracts or committing to business deals during a retrograde phase. It is an appropriate time for planning to launch new endeavors after the retrograde cycle completes.

24 Thursday ~ First Quarter Moon in Sagittarius 9:57

Taking a broader approach to life draws balance and stability into your surroundings. It enables energy to flow and offers new possibilities that tempt you forward. New ideas are incoming that help you grow your talents and cultivate abilities that provide advancement. The more you get involved with developing your life, the broader your perception is of what is achievable. It brings new pathways that offer rising prospects and growth.

AUGUST

25 Friday ~ Mars trine Pluto 12:22

Today's aspect offers rising prospects for your career. It brings a goal-orientated, disciplined, and centered focus on improving your working life. It is a highly creative process that represents a new beginning. Growing your talents and refining your abilities helps you develop a remarkable trajectory forward for your working life. Being proactive, determined, and resourceful cracks the code to a brighter chapter. A new role looms overhead for your working life.

26 Saturday

An invitation to mingle draws an opportunity that feels like a good fit for your lifestyle. It initiates a time of progress and growth. You land in an active and productive environment that helps you accomplish much in a group environment. An emphasis on improving the elements in your life sees potential pick-up steam. Getting involved with expanding your social life draws dividends as it links you to new possibilities.

27 Sunday ~ Sun opposed Saturn 8:28, Mars ingress Libra r 13:15

Something percolating in the background of your life soon appears to tempt you forward. An exciting possibility makes a dashing entrance into your life. It heightens confidence and builds a sense of purpose that lets you use your talents to elevate the potential around your life. Life-affirming possibilities connect you with others who offer a web of support. It brings a chance for collaboration, growth, and kinship.

AUGUST

28 Monday

A new cycle emerges in your life that launches an exciting direction. It brings change and opportunity flowing into your world. A time of creativity and innovation helps build your talents and advance skills in new areas. As you transition towards unique possibilities that promote growth, you make notable tracks on growing your career path. Remarkable changes on the horizon give you the green light to expand your life.

29 Tuesday ~ Uranus turns Retrograde in Taurus 2:11

Uranus moving into a retrograde phase boosts idealism; it offers big sky pictures that help motivate change to improve the world around you. This planetary cycle will boost your confidence and foster leadership qualities. It deepens initiative and offers a fresh wind that spurs creativity and an uptick of potential. Your search to improve your circumstances unearths valid leads that cultivate growth and rising prospects.

30 Wednesday

New potential ignites your imagination and leads to a chapter that sparks growth. You gain a boost when you hear the whispers of a new role that offers progression. Overall, the landscape ahead is expanding, promoting rising prospects that help you dive into a new area. It brings an exciting and active time that makes you enthusiastic about future possibilities. Your life gets a boost when news arrives that opens the door to a path you can expand.

31 Thursday ~ Super Moon, Blue Full Moon in Pisces 1:36

You are reaching the end of a cycle. It is essential to take the time required to rebalance your energy as you close the door to the past. Ahead, life brings curious changes that enable you to switch directions. It brings a journey that promotes excitement as you nurture your dreams. Honing in on this potential clears the slate and attracts happiness to your social life. It brings a lively and engaging time with friends.

SEPTEMBER

Sun	Mon	Tue	Wed	Thu	Fri	Sat
					1	2
3	4	5	6	7	8	9
10	11	12	13	14	15	16
17	18	19	20	21	22	23
24	25	26	27	28	29	30

wild
SOUL

New Moon

Corn/Harvest Moon

September

1 Friday

Your dedication and perseverance help you turn a corner and enter a winning streak. A time of blossoming activity begins a journey filled with hope and promise. Upgrading your skills cracks the code to rising prospects in your career path. An emphasis on improving your life creates a bridge towards a more secure future. It helps you launch into a progressive chapter of developing plans.

2 Saturday

Information arrives that shines a light on unique goals. Increasing freedom and adventure are on the horizon, tempting you towards lush green pastures. The seeds planted during this time blossom into a happy journey towards growing your life in a new direction. Adding fuel to motivation sees inspiration skyrocket. Branching out and growing your talents in a new area opens the gate to transformation.

3 Sunday

Freedom and expansion come calling to dust off the doldrums and create sparks of creativity and potential in your life. Life is about to become busier as the pace picks up and focuses on expansion. The essence of manifestation helps you craft plans for future growth. It brings a social aspect that adds glamour and possibility to your life. News arrives that releases the heaviness and helps transform your vision.

SEPTEMBER

4 Monday ~ Labor Day, Venus turns direct in Leo 1:19, Mercury trine Jupiter 10:29, Jupiter turns Retrograde in Taurus 14:14

Venus turns direct and brings an open road of potential into your love life. Confidence rises and empowers you to lead from your most authentic place. Increasing possibilities leave you feeling optimistic as changes ahead attract refreshing potential. News arrives that propels you towards a journey of promise and romance. Sharing thoughtful conversations replenishes emotional tanks.

5 Tuesday

You can take advantage of positive energy that heightens creativity. It prepares you to develop a new idea or project that crosses your path. You quickly move through the planning stage and create a brilliant option that offers fantastic results. Concentrating on nurturing your life lets you blaze a trail towards a successful outcome. It connects you with knowledgeable people who share thoughtful ideas. It offers a shift in priorities as you get busy with new goals.

6 Wednesday ~ Sun conjunct Mercury 11: 08, Last Quarter Moon in Gemini 22:21

Independent thinking and innovative ideas can be attributed to the Sun and Mercury conjunct today. You discover further leads that bring forward momentum into your life. Developing your abilities and nurturing your talents bring change and advancement into view. It transpires into a journey that offers room to advance your gifts into a new area. Working with your skills initiates an enterprising chapter that involves higher learning.

7 Thursday

Life lights up with new options. You can take a deep breath and dive into the deep end as you are supported to grow your world. It helps you propel your skills forward and achieve the growth you seek in your working life. Things fall into place as new chapter ushers in a happy time for developing your talents and growing your world. It begins a highly productive journey that becomes a source of happiness and inspiration.

September

8 Friday ~ Sun trine Jupiter 11:12

The Sun forms a trine with Jupiter, which increases good luck and fortune in your life. A positive influence nurtures beneficial outcomes. It marks a freedom-driven time that captures the essence of creativity. Life expands outwardly, which clears the way toward an active and happy chapter of networking with friends. You strike gold by expanding your circle of friends as it lets you turn a corner and head into a winning chapter of nurturing companionship.

9 Saturday

A lucky break brings a valuable opportunity that feeds your soul. It benefits your life on several levels as energy improves, and you feel happier and more optimistic about the potential in your world. An endeavor you develop will progress and keep life humming as you engage in projects and areas that capture your inspiration. Your ability to work towards a plan produces an abundant harvest that enriches life.

10 Sunday

Energizing information cracks the code to a brighter chapter. It highlights nurturing creativity and sharing your abilities with a broader audience. It offers a social aspect that connects you with like-minded people ready to engage in discussions and collaborations. A change of scene ahead helps you move towards a productive time of expanding your life in an increasingly prosperous direction.

September

11 Monday

Life brings an opportunity to learn and prosper. Growing your abilities opens an expressive and expansive journey that nurtures your skills. You discover hidden pathways that hold curious options for your life. You soon create a bridge towards greener pastures that marks the start of growing your world. It brings a busy time that lets you embark on launching your talents higher. Refining your talents and creative skills opens the floodgates of rising potential.

12 Tuesday

You crack the code to a brighter phase when information crosses your path, drawing excitement. It allows you to flex your talents and use your abilities in a progressive arena. Advancing your skills by incorporating innovative techniques enables you to achieve a successful result. The pressure eases as you light up pathways of growth and prosperity. Success is on the horizon, seeing inspiration surging in your world.

13 Wednesday

An outstanding opportunity arrives, which helps advance life into an enterprising area. It helps release restrictions and limitations as you put delays behind you and get involved with planning an ambitious project. Unleashing your talents draws progression around your career path. It brings a surge of opportunities that offer rising prospects as you turn the corner and head towards advancement.

14 Thursday

Life brings remarkable opportunities that set you on a refreshing trend to grow your world. It helps you create a strong foundation that offers room to progress life forward into new areas. Being receptive to change attracts options that facilitate growth, learning, and advancement. Fortune aligns to form a clear window of opportunity that expands your horizons. Dabbling in growing your skills draws a pleasing result.

SEPTEMBER

15 Friday ~ Rosh Hashanah (begins at sunset), New Moon in Virgo 1:40, Mercury turns direct at 20:20

Mercury turns direct, and this improves communication and interpersonal bonds. It offers a renewed interest in your social life that helps harmonize the frazzled tensions during the retrograde phase. News arrives that illuminates a journey of abundance, happiness, and companionship. It brings a sense of connection into focus as you blaze a trail towards a remarkable destination.

16 Saturday ~ Sun trine Uranus 1:23

Today, the Sun trine Uranus aspect adds a dash of spontaneity and excitement into your life. It is a favorable aspect that brings the freedom-driven chapter to light. Focusing on your social life draws a pleasing result as you connect with kindred spirits who offer excitement and passion. It tips the scales in your favor. It brings warmth to your social life as in-depth discussions blaze a trail toward new areas.

17 Sunday ~ Rosh Hashanah (ends at sunset), Venus square Jupiter 6:12

The Venus square Jupiter aspect makes it the perfect day for unwinding and relaxing with your social circle. An easygoing vibe draws thoughtful conversations, and contemplating options draws clarity into future goals. Setting intentions lets you gather your resources before you prepare to develop the journey ahead. It brings a social aspect that connects you with others who offer advice and wisdom.

SEPTEMBER

18 Monday

You lift the lid on an enterprising chapter that grows your abilities and refines your skills. Research and planning the path help you place your best foot forward. Developing your talents lights the way towards a prestigious area that brings a boost to your working goals. It rules advancing life towards new endeavors as you achieve an active growth phase in your working life. It opens rising prospects that nurture more security in your life.

19 Tuesday ~ Sun opposed Neptune 11:17

Your perception broadens as the Sun lights up Neptune's dreamy aspects. Engaging with creativity and imagination draws rising ideas and innovative concepts to consider. Being open to change and adaptable to new possibilities gives you free rein to harness your creativity and dive into growing areas that feel sublime. It takes you toward a brighter, lighter chapter and is in tune with your spirit.

20 Wednesday

Developing your unique skills and talents links you up with positive change. Laying the groundwork for expansion one brick at a time fortifies foundations and gives you a strong basis from which to grow your world. You connect with inspiration, giving you the green light to develop your abilities and head towards growth and learning. Developments ahead bring news and potential flowing into your life. It brings the right environment to explore advancement.

21 Thursday ~ International Day of Peace, Sun trine Pluto 5:20

Moving in alignment with your instincts is a positive way to grow your world. It helps you progress with personal goals as you commit to prioritizing yourself. Information arrives that offers a new direction for your life. It promotes a time of expansion and adventure that lifts the lid on an inspiring time ahead. It kickstarts a creative and pioneering journey that nurtures your abilities and grows your talents.

SEPTEMBER

22 Friday ~ Sun ingress Libra 6:46, First Quarter Moon in Sagittarius 19:32, Mercury at Greatest Elongation 17.9W

You enter a productive time that helps you cook up a storm with friends. It attracts invitations and activities that cultivate happiness and increase your drive and sense of purpose. You hear of a happy surprise that draws excitement and joy. Being adaptable helps you change plans on a dime and make the most of a sudden invitation.

23 Saturday ~ Mabon/Fall Equinox 6:50

The more you uncover about your life, the more you feel the energy of the past surrounding your life. You reveal secret information that helps you understand your life more profoundly. The insight you gain fuels creativity and brings expansion to the forefront of your life. It adds a unique element to your life that nurtures well-being and harmony. Building grounded foundations draw a secure environment on the home front.

24 Sunday ~ Yom Kippur (begins at sunset)

Increasing activity around your social life leads to developments and new potential. It attracts new friends, and this dynamic environment hits the ticket for a happy chapter of mingling and networking. You have a flair for bringing people together and sharing thoughts and ideas. Information arrives that launches a bold shift forward in your social environment. It underscores the energy of magic that surrounds your life at this time.

September

25 Monday ~ Yom Kippur (ends at sunset), Mercury trine Jupiter 12:12

Today's Mercury trine Jupiter aspect brings optimism and good news. Research, learning, study, and socializing are favored. This trine is ideal for formulating new plans and engaging in future-orientated brainstorming sessions. It's also the perfect time to sort and organize; your office, workspace, closet, or even your whole life. It brings the gift of stability, providing a grounded foundation as you grow your options and develop goals.

26 Tuesday

You touch down on a landscape filled with new potential. It offers room to develop your abilities as you take on unique assignments that showcase talents and illuminate pathways for sharing your skills with a broader audience. A positive influence ahead transitions you towards learning new areas. You find your groove as you expand life outwardly and thrive in a more vibrant landscape.

27 Wednesday

An area you become involved with brings essential changes flowing into your life. Being open to new people and possibilities helps you manifest a fresh start. Lovely changes flow into your world that offers expansion and growth. Nurturing your social life draws dividends as it brings a meaningful shift forward that opens a path toward exciting adventures. It helps you break fresh ground as new possibilities come knocking.

28 Thursday

News arrives that brings the winds of inspiration and motivation to your door. This information lets you lift the lid on a journey that beckons you to develop your skills. It offers a productive journey that grows your abilities and nurtures your talents. It brings an area that offers progression, advancement, and growth. Directing your energy into developing this project sets the stage to improve life. You transition onto a path that provides an uptick of potential.

October

Sun	Mon	Tue	Wed	Thu	Fri	Sat
1	2	3	4	5	6	7
8	9	10	11	12	13	14
15	16	17	18	19	20	21
22	23	24	25	26	27	28
29	30	31				

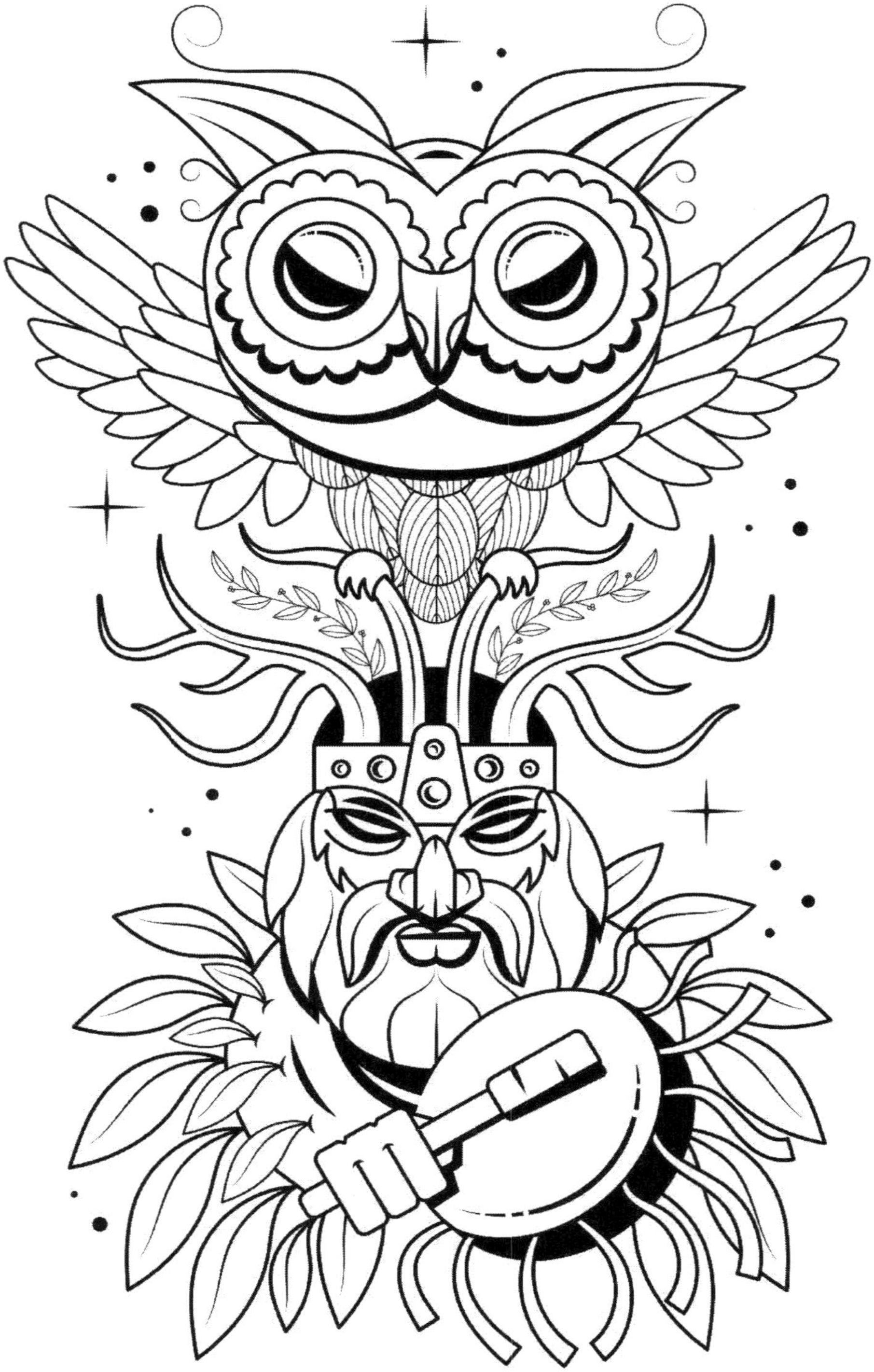

New Moon

Hunters Moon

September/October

29 Friday ~ Sukkot (begins at sunset), Super Moon, Corn Moon, Harvest Full Moon in Aries 9:58, Venus square Uranus 17:53

A restless vibe caused by a Venus Uranus square could undermine the security in your love life or the broader social environment if you are single. A freedom-loving vibration makes you want to be spontaneous and engage in unique adventures that change the day-to-day routine of your life. You discover a dynamic and active environment filled with stimulating conversations.

30 Saturday ~Mercury trine Uranus 16:56

Today's trine is perfect for using technology to keep life supported and flowing in your social life. Communication is your passageway to a more connected social life. Being innovative and thinking outside the box connects you with diverse pathways of growth and expansion. It removes the roadblocks and opens a path that cultivates engaging and unique friendships. Expanding options see you circulating more often with friends and kindred spirits.

1 Sunday

Your river of hopes and dreams merge with a sea of understanding about the path ahead. It brings goals that make your life a priority. It focuses on developing your world in alignment with the person you are currently becoming. Life becomes a blaze of activity and opportunity. The power of magic stimulates creative growth and lets you manifest rewarding outcomes. Rising creativity beautifully accents your life with new possibilities.

OCTOBER

2 Monday ~ Mercury opposed Neptune 3:34

The Mercury and Neptune opposition helps you communicate your ideas and thoughts today. However, you may find work challenging as rising creativity brings a desire to daydream. It does see you heading towards change as you reveal hidden depths of insight that enable progress to occur. Removing the confusion allows for a unique journey to blossom. Nurturing your dreams and goals lights the path towards developing skills.

3 Tuesday ~ Mercury trine Pluto 19:20

News arrives that is a catalyst for change. It brings a unique pathway that lets you harness your adaptability and head toward growth. Imagination and creative thinking rise to the challenge as increasing luck advances life to greener pastures. You take in an environment that is ripe with blessings and potential. Entering a cycle of increasing prosperity motivates you to expand the barriers and take on an ambitious project.

4 Wednesday

New information lets you gain traction on developing an exciting goal. A cycle of increasing abundance marks a time of magic and excitement. Life becomes active and progressive. A new area comes calling and draws a path that reflects your current hopes and dreams. It lets you sail on a timely voyage towards growing your abilities and working with your talents. It offers ample time that reinvents potential and brings a transition into your life.

5 Thursday ~ Mercury ingress Libra 12:06

Mercury can bring an indecisive vibe that causes stagnant energy. Procrastination can be an issue that delays progress in the workplace. Removing distractions and streamlining your environment can help mitigate the effect of this transit. You can cut away from limitations and open the gate on a journey that takes your skills to the next level. Libra attracts balanced energy, helping you find a middle path through your day.

OCTOBER

6 Friday ~ Sukkot (ends at sunset), Last Quarter Moon in Cancer 13:48

Your fortune is on the rise as an uptick of potential surrounds you. It brings the ideal opportunity to embrace a change of pace and engage with a broader world of potential which lies just outside your door. A friend hopes to sync up with you, and getting involved with your social life bolsters your mood and draws well-being into your world. You discover that enjoying a freedom-driven chapter is the antidote for the doldrums.

7 Saturday ~ Draconids Meteor Shower. Oct 6-10

The changes ahead bring new options into your life that let you unpack a chapter that offers room to grow your world. A cluster of activities brings new possibilities into your social life. Your willingness to be open to new people and experiences brings you golden moments. Creativity burns brightly and connects you with others with similar takes on life. It offers a time of lively conversations that focus on entertaining and relaxing with friends.

8 Sunday

A colorful chapter ahead nurtures stable and happy foundations in your home life. Focusing on improving the energy around your situation draws stability and progress into your world. It lets you bid farewell to setbacks and issues as you enter a busy time of positive distractions. It does bring a chance to mingle, and spontaneous invitations see you acting on impulse. It translates to an outstanding phase of sharing with loved ones and enjoying all life offers.

October

9 Monday ~ Thanksgiving Day (Canada), Indigenous People's Day, Columbus Day, Mars square Pluto 1:04, Venus ingress Virgo 1:06

You discover many creative people are in your broader circle of friends; a networking opportunity aligns your energy with lively discussions and thoughtful dialogues. An undercurrent of unique potential helps you thrive in a vibrant and dynamic environment. Well-crafted ideas underscore the essence of magic and manifestation in your world.

10 Tuesday ~ Venus opposed Saturn at 6:11. Pluto turns direct at 11:43

Opportunities ahead bring a newfound endeavor that is a source of inspiration. It brings motivation, creativity, and growth to the forefront of your life. It lets you banish cobwebs and enter a time of progress and rising prospects. Working with your abilities shines a light on using your talents to expand your life outwardly. It sets the stage to research, learn, and grow in a remarkable area. A vibrant landscape revolutionizes the potential possible in your world.

11 Wednesday

A wave of information initiates a phase of growth and evolution for your career path. It lets you dip your toes into a new area as you extend your reach and advance your skills. It helps you create a grounded basis that progresses your skills while making the most of your talents. It brings an option ripe for development that moves you in alignment with the person you are becoming. Developing your life kicks off an ambitious venture worth your time.

12 Thursday ~ Mars ingress Scorpio 3:59

Methodically exploring new options for your life helps you unearth a lead worth further investigation. You discover a unique pathway that offers growth and cultivates growing your talents. Life is ready to bloom. Keeping open to expanding your horizons draws good results into your life. It lets you gain a footing in a more grounded and stable direction. Channeling excess energy into this area brings a journey that sparks growth, learning, and happiness.

OCTOBER

13 Friday ~ Mars trine Saturn 12:28

The Mars trine Saturn aspect today boosts your working life. It enables you to gain traction on achieving a successful result. It puts the finishing touches on your working week as you easily meet deadlines. This robust transit gives you the strength, ambition, and perseverance to take on the most complex tasks and complete them on time. Increased productivity and efficiency get the job done. Your self-discipline keeps you focused without being distracted or discouraged.

14 Saturday ~ New Moon in Libra 17:54, Annular Solar Eclipse 17:59

You enter clearer skies and can embrace circulating with your wider social environment. Mingling in the community connects you to a refreshing level of abundance. Exchanging thoughts with kindred spirits expands your social life and rejuvenates your soul. News arrives that helps you release the heaviness and transform your vision towards a lighter chapter. Change is in the air, bringing an enriching time that brims with potential.

15 Sunday

Life moves forward towards a social aspect that offers a chance to mingle. It relieves the pressure and creates an environment that stimulates your mind and provides a sense of connection and well-being. Getting involved with your circle of friends draws expansion into your life. It does bring lively discussions and the energy of rejuvenation into your world. A happy time ahead brings grounded and secure power into your foundations.

OCTOBER

16 Monday

A bold new beginning emerges in your life soon. It brings a transition that offers forward momentum. It connects you with others who are also on a similar path. Refining your skills lets you develop an exciting and unique journey that advances life forward towards rising prospects. Moving in alignment with your passions lays the groundwork to grow your world outwardly. Your willingness to explore leads brings golden opportunities to light.

17 Tuesday

A wave of opportunities breaks upon your shore and encourages you to head towards new horizons. A new option anchors your energy in a project that offers a chance to launch your star to a lofty height. Self-expression and creativity are rising, boosting confidence, and expanding your life. A river of awareness cultivates self-development and rules advancement in an area that inspires you on an emotional level.

18 Wednesday

An avenue opens that draws lighter energy into your life. It brings a time of nurturing your home environment and improving the options in your world. It marks a slower pace that restores harmony and equilibrium. It helps you lay the groundwork to improve the foundations in your world. Focusing on the building blocks lets you make essential changes that progress life towards new possibilities and options.

19 Thursday

Life ahead brings opportunities for creativity and self-expression. It brings potential flowing into your world that nurtures expansion. Information arrives out of the blue; it feels specifically for you. It gets a chance to grow your talents in a new area, which soon becomes a strong focus for you moving forward. It connects you with kindred spirits who offer social support and friendship. It places you in the box seat to form new friends as it widens your social circle.

OCTOBER

20 Friday ~ Sun conjunct Mercury 5:37

In conjunction with Mercury, the Sun is a favorable aspect that attracts communication. It is the best of all elements for receiving or sending communication. Interacting with others is vital today. It stimulates your need to share ideas and engage in thoughtful discussions that nurture well-being and harmony in your life. Mingling and networking draw a productive and lively environment.

21 Saturday ~ Orionids Meteor Shower Oct 2nd – Nov 7th, Mercury square Pluto 12:50, Sun square Pluto 14:09

Today's aspect causes a challenging environment as you find your judgment or authority tested. Being challenged and tested feels uncomfortable as you think you are making the right choices and decisions for your life. The Mercury square Pluto transit also attracts interactions with other people who feed the gossip mill and cultivate drama, leading to a toxic environment.

22 Sunday ~ First Quarter Moon in Aquarius 03:29, Venus trine Jupiter 4:32, Mercury ingress Scorpio 6:46, Mercury trine Saturn 16:12

The Venus trine Jupiter aspect offers golden threads around your social and love life. It is one of the most anticipated transits which harmonizes interpersonal bonds and offers rising prospects of good luck to your romantic life. It is fascinating to those seeking love or wanting a deeper romantic bond. Thoughtful conversations and expressive gestures promote happiness and well-being.

OCTOBER

23 Monday ~ Venus at Greatest Elongation 46.4W, Sun ingress Scorpio 16:17

Your career heads toward growth as an upswing of potential let you step out on a journey that expands your talents. It offers a fruitful time for working with your abilities as you find progression occurs quickly during this time. As you gain traction on developing your goals, you discover your situation is evolving, broadening your reach and enabling you to climb the ladder towards success. Deepening your knowledge offers impressive results.

24 Tuesday ~ Sun trine Saturn 7:13

Today's Sun, Saturn trine, gives you a commanding presence in the workplace. Confidence peaks in mid-afternoon, enabling you to effectively manage the day's tasks with relative ease as your energy keeps humming along productively. You conquer the workload and achieve a robust result with your consistent and disciplined efforts, which draw a pleasing effect and the added benefits of increased job satisfaction.

25 Wednesday

You are on the cusp of change regarding growing your career. A growth-driven phase ahead opens new pathways. It brings a learning time as you get involved with deepening your knowledge and refining your skills. A clear goal comes into focus, and creating a strategic plan maps out the stepping stones to building a path towards success. A role you become involved in developing takes flight and heads towards rising prospects.

26 Thursday

In a happy development, an invitation arrives that brings a chance to mingle. Connecting with others in your circle of friends nurtures your spirit. It draws an engaging chapter on sharing ideas and thoughts. It emphasizes improving interpersonal ties. Spending more time with friends and companions lights a path forward towards growing your world outwardly. It sparks conversations that draw rising prospects into your life.

OCTOBER

27 Friday

A crossroads ahead bring a turning point that enables you to cut away from areas that failed to achieve fruition. It also points you in the correct direction to improve the circumstances. It brings a happy chapter that opens a flurry of excitement as you embark on new adventures in your social life. You blaze through a time of lively and engaging interactions which inspire change.

28 Saturday ~ Mars opposed Jupiter 16: 03, Hunters Full Moon in Taurus 20:23 Partial Lunar Eclipse 20:14

You can embrace one of the luckiest aspects today when Mars opposes Jupiter and draws good fortune into your life. The winds of change carry news information into your surroundings. Today's transit increases your self-confidence and ability to handle your time and energy demands. It brings a competitive edge that fuels ambitions and the desire to achieve your goals.

29 Sunday ~ Mercury opposed Jupiter 3:44, Mercury conjunct Mars 14:21

Today, Mercury is the show's star and draws a favorable aspect that nurtures good fortune in your social life. It brings a chance to share with friends and loved ones. Relaxing and unwinding enable you to restore frazzled nerves and build robust foundations. Indeed, focusing on nourishing your foundations will help you move toward greener pastures. It marks a time of increasing opportunities for your social life that nurture happiness.

NOVEMBER

Sun	Mon	Tue	Wed	Thu	Fri	Sat
			1	2	3	4
5	6	7	8	9	10	11
12	13	14	15	16	17	18
19	20	21	22	23	24	25
26	27	28	29	30		

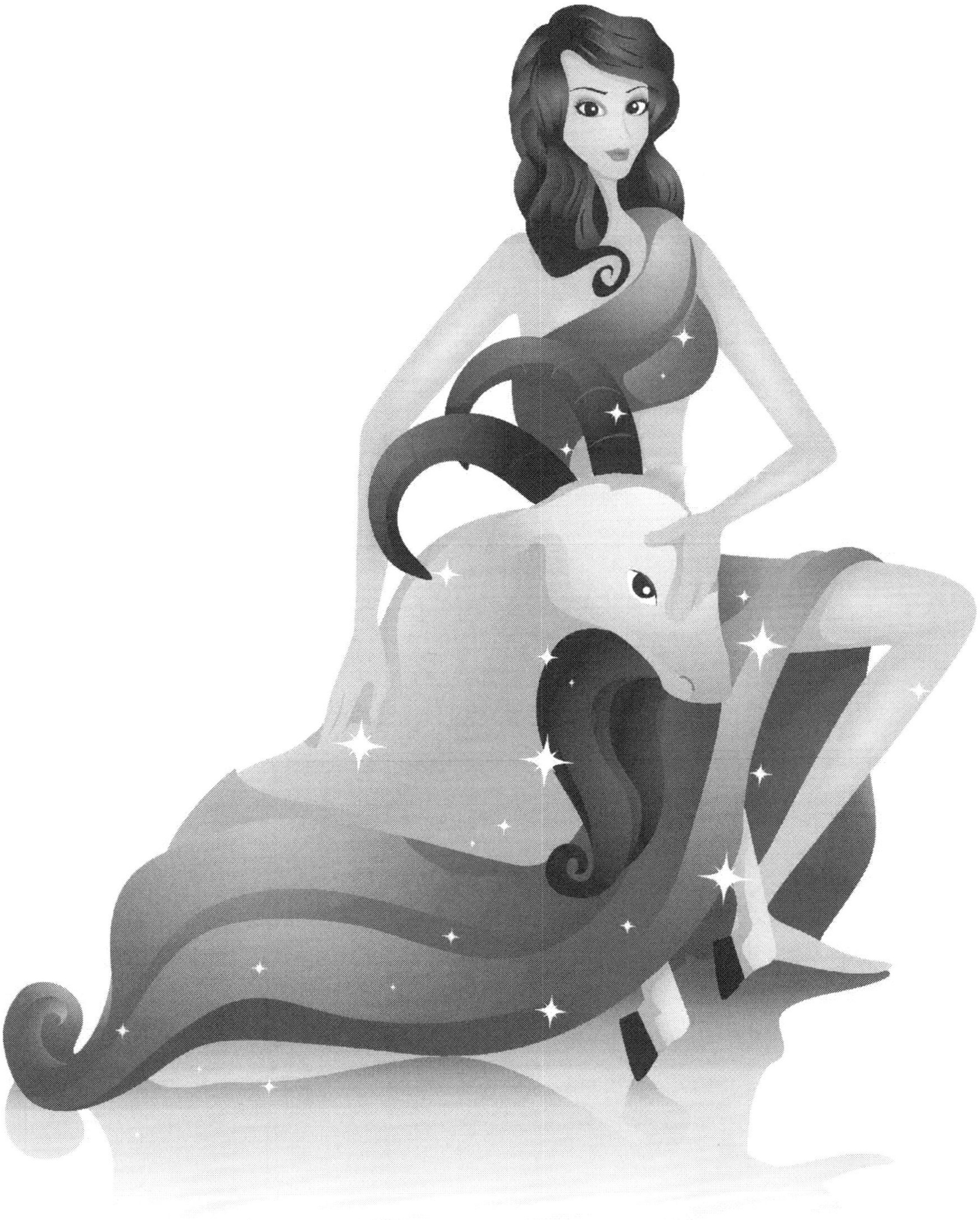

New Moon

Beaver Moon

October/November

30 Monday

Unexpected invitations chart a course towards a more social environment. It brings opportunities to mingle, promoting a positive trend that nurtures well-being and harmony. An emphasis on improving your situation draws transformation and change into your world. It releases worries and dials down the stress as you explore an enticing landscape of possibilities. It brings a chance to network with others who nurture your life on many levels.

31 Tuesday ~ Samhain/Halloween, All Hallows Eve Venus trine Uranus 12:51

Embrace a magical and vibrant Halloween under the influence of an engaging and dynamic Venus trine Uranus aspect that adds a dash of spontaneity and fun into your life. This unique aspect brings curious people into your life. It lets you pick up the threads of manifestation and weave a basket of supportive connections that offer growth and support. A positive influence brings an enriching phase that promotes happiness and harmony.

1 Wednesday ~ All Saints' Day

Focusing on the building blocks of your life takes you towards a little worn track. This path nurtures your skills and elevates your abilities in a curious area. It helps you take the first steps on a journey that holds meaning. It gives you the green light to connect with inspiration and pour your energy into developing your talents. Harnessing your creativity cracks the code to transform life as you create new possibilities.

2 Thursday

Being highly flexible, adaptable, and open enables you to make the most of the changes ahead. Keeping your eyes on the path onward lets you pivot away from trouble and embark on growing your world outwardly. Changes arrive that can feel unsettling, but it enables you to restore balance and remove the outworn layers of your life. A leap of faith reveals a possibility that sparks inspiration. Reawakening to the creativity within your spirit draws motivation to succeed.

NOVEMBER

3 Friday ~ Sun opposed Jupiter at 5:02. Venus opposed Neptune at 22:05

The Sun opposed to Jupiter, brings the increasing potential for wealth and good fortune. Rising prospects see things in your life fall in place as you turn a corner and head towards a lucky streak. Significant change brings a chapter that empowers and enriches your life. Being proactive draws a pleasing result as swift improvements follow the expansion of horizons around your life. You ramp up the potential possible by being flexible and adaptive to change.

4 Saturday ~ Taurids Meteor Shower. Sept 7th - Dec 10th
Saturn turns direct in Pisces at 7:15. Mercury opposed Uranus at 16:06

The Mercury opposed Uranus transit bringing a chaotic and hectic pace. The busier pace may leave you feeling tense, anxious, and scattered. Uranus adds a dash of the unexpected, leaving you scrambling to deal with surprise news. Information emerges from the left field, leaving you wondering what will happen next. Focusing on the basics improves balance.

5 Sunday ~ Last Quarter Moon in Leo 08:37

News arrives that opens pathways in your social life. It brings an invitation to your door that enables you to connect in a community environment. Mingling with others draws new people into your circle of friends. It opens a time that expands your life, bringing a changing scene on the horizon. This dynamic environment leaves you feeling optimistic about future possibilities. It lights a way towards abundance and happiness.

November

6 Monday ~ Venus trine Pluto 14:38

Today's Venus trine with Pluto adds intensity to your love life. This aspect turns up the heat in your personal life. Sexual attraction and passion rise as you get busy developing your personal life. Singles will likely find new romance soon, while couples can embrace a more connected and sizzling love life. Attractive options bring a bounty of potential, and sharing thoughtful discussions promote rising possibilities for romance and companionship.

7 Tuesday ~ Mercury trine Neptune 1:36

Creativity, imagination, and innovation blaze a wildfire of inspiration as Mercury and Neptune form a trine today. Increased sensitivity to this vibrational energy attracts a boost into your world that bolsters vitality. It offers a dramatic shift that helps you quickly learn or develop a new area. An option arrives that enables you to push back the barriers and expand your horizons. It opens the doors to developing unique dreams that nurture your life.

8 Wednesday ~ Venus ingress Libra 9:27

Lively discussions with friends and companions attract a productive and engaging environment. Curious news arrives that offers insight into the path ahead. Setting goals and developing a plan enables you to grow your world outwardly. Communication comes, which opens the floodgates to socializing. It brings a busy time for creating positive outcomes by sharing thoughtful discussions that nurture creativity and unique ideas.

9 Thursday ~ Mercury sextile Pluto 12:16

Today, the Mercury sextile Pluto transit adds extra layers and dimensions to your creative thinking. It brings an ideal time for research, planning, and mapping out unique areas for future development. Your penetrating inquiries delve deep and help you discover potential pitfalls and issues. Your inquiring mind places you in a solid position to grow your dreams as you do due diligence and understand all aspects of your investigations.

November

10 Friday ~ Veterans Day (Observed), Mercury ingress Sagittarius 6:22, Mercury square Saturn 15:07

Today's Mercury square Saturn challenges critical thinking skills and intrepid enquiring. Tensions could flare up and lead to disruptions. Miscommunication is more likely when you are not on the same page as the person you talk to about your thoughts and ideas. This transit brings a chance to focus on harmonizing sensitive triggers. Channeling your inner Zen is your best move forward today.

11 Saturday ~ Veterans Day, Remembrance Day (Canada), Mars opposed Uranus 21:11

The Mars opposed Uranus could catch you off guard today, leading to tension in personal bonds. An unexpected tension could flare up, causing an argument or dispute with a family member or loved one. Yesterday's transit compounds the issue as it added a layer of complexity to communication in your life. More Zen moves are needed today.

12 Sunday

Cultivating your social life brings fulfillment as it opens a path toward rising possibilities. There is a great deal of abundance swirling around the periphery of your broader circle of friends. Opportunities to mingle let you connect with people you haven't seen for a while. A social aspect ahead lights up pathways of companionship. It gives you the green light to focus on building stable foundations in your social life.

NOVEMBER

13 Monday ~ New Moon in Scorpio 09:27, Sun opposed Uranus 17:20

The Sun opposed Uranus transit attracts a restless vibe that gives you the green light to try something new and different. It drives a liberating chapter that offers spontaneity as you get busy expressing your unique individual melody and personality. You arrive at a gateway that opens to a brighter future. It draws an energizing time to take control of the reins and make pivotal changes to improve your situation.

14 Tuesday

Building stable foundations in your world, remove the cobwebs as it helps you move forward with purpose. As you progress toward improving your circumstances, you lift the lid on a chapter that brings new potential into your world. It is wise to invest in yourself. Your creative expression abilities emphasize growing your life in alignment with your spirit. It brings a chance to join forces with other supportive companions.

15 Wednesday ~ Mercury sextile Venus 12:47

A loving vibe helps you get past hump day. Today's Mercury sextile Venus adds a positive influence that harmonizes and nurtures well-being in your world. Less stress and more enjoyment grow solid foundations. Personal relationships benefit from open communication leading to fulfillment. A sense of kinship and companionship nurtures the foundations of your life. It brings the sharing of thoughtful dialogues and entertaining discussions.

16 Thursday

Opportunities in the workplace draw an active time that offers growth and prosperity. It opens your life to a broader bounty of possibility as an opportunity comes knocking, and this gives you an exciting sign that things are shifting forward in your life. Newfound motivation fuels inspiration and enables you to launch into a chapter of gain and progression. Life is ripe with remarkable possibilities worthy of development.

November

17 Friday ~ Leonids Meteor Shower November 6-30ᵗʰ, Mars trine Neptune 8:36, Sun trine Neptune 14:51

Under the influence of Neptune, creativity soars, epiphany's and lightbulb moments are the order of the day. Your abilities take center stage as you chart a course towards developing goals. A curious assignment ahead draws excitement and optimism. As motivation increases, you soon feel the lightness returning full force, and you chart a course toward progress and advancement.

18 Saturday ~ Sun conjunct Mars 5:41

Sun conjunct Mars brings abundant energy and initiative, and your drive to try new things increases. A desire for action can cause restlessness if not channeled and released. It marks a lovely rhythm that sees the pace of life pick up steam. You tap into a journey that inspires change, and it has you feeling optimistic about prospects. It emphasizes a time of fresh beginnings that connects you with a happy and enterprising landscape.

19 Sunday

Life up ahead supports your efforts by improving the foundations of your life. It draws lighter energy that nourishes well-being and renewal. It refreshes the potential around your home and social life. It links up with an expressive and expansive time that rules spontaneous get-togethers and opportunities to mingle. It brings a journey that focuses on friendships and companions. Lively discussions bring insightful ideas to light.

November

20 Monday ~ First Quarter Moon in Aquarius 10:50, Sun sextile Pluto 21:26

Today's Sun sextile Pluto transit drives ambitions and sees you heading into the working week with an increased drive to succeed and conquer your goals. Feeling determined and purposeful enables you to nail your tasks quickly and finish work with energy still in the tank. You discover you can truly thrive in a unique and dynamic landscape. An original and innovative journey rules the way of advancement in your working life as you take on a new learning area.

21 Tuesday

A sweet opportunity emerges that has you thinking big about future possibilities. It tempts you forward and involves a degree of research and planning to capitalize on the highest potential possible in this area. It brings a chance to collaborate and join forces with a kindred spirit which adds a dash of magic and creative genius. It brings growth that establishes your talents in a new arena. It offers a lucrative path forward in your life.

22 Wednesday ~ Mars sextile Pluto 1:17, Sun ingress Sagittarius 13:59

Today's transit increases energy in the workplace. No job is too small as you take on the lot and work towards your vision. Indeed, new opportunities are incoming that take your talents to the next level. Streamlining and refining the path ahead offers a productive and growth-orientated journey that elevates your abilities. Creativity and inspiration raise the bar of what is possible in your life when you stay open to new options and possibilities.

23 Thursday ~ Thanksgiving Day (USA), Sun square Saturn 9:46

Saturn is the ruler of honoring traditions and following rigid structures that form set boundaries. Today's square illuminates a happy time shared with loved ones, perfect with Saturn, who delights in honoring the past. An optimistic outlook attracts like-minded people into your sphere. A social aspect helps you embrace new adventures in your life. Opportunities to mingle draw fruitful results. It connects you with companions who offer light and harmony.

November

24 Friday ~ Mars ingress Sagittarius 10:10

This transit emits a rebellious vibe that rejuvenates your energy and has you seeking expansion. Inspiring conversations with thoughtful companions nurture lead to happiness in your social life. It charts a course towards an enriching chapter that ushers in social engagement, laughter, and thoughtful discussions. Being open to change underscores your willingness to improve your circumstances through the choices and decisions you make in your life.

25 Saturday ~ Mars square Saturn 16:57

Today's aspect can feel challenging as your mind is on Saturn's to-do list. You may find it difficult to relax and unwind when your thoughts turn to the irons you have burning in the fire. Your creativity and inspiration burn brightly, opening up a treasure box of potential pathways. It brings a time of planning and developing your dreams and aspirations. You enter a winning time that attracts a cycle of growth.

26 Sunday

Exciting news ahead brings potential to your social circle. It brings a busy time that emphasizes building security and improving interpersonal ties. It offers an abundant chapter that grows dreams as you create a vital shift forward in your life. Sweeping changes on the horizon draw growth and prosperity into your world. It brings a time of socializing that nurtures stable foundations in your life.

November

27 Monday ~ Beaver Full Moon in Gemini 09:16, Mercury square Neptune 13:26

Today, the Mercury square Neptune aspect can distort or make mountains of molehills. It adds a dash of illusion into your business dealings that can have your head spinning with tall tales and trying to sort the truth from exaggeration. If someone disingenuous crosses your path today, don't fall for these ploys, as desperate sales tactics will not sit well for you during this transit. The Full Moon brings an opportune time to heal sensitive areas in your life.

28 Tuesday

Being in sync with your vision for future growth draws better results. You uncover information that helps create exceptional progress. Well-crafted ideas are soon launched into the stratosphere, enabling you to develop your skills. Being open to side options helps develop unique goals that grow your abilities. Doing research and planning helps map out potential areas for development next year. Life rewards on many levels as you uncover intriguing leads.

29 Wednesday

Your willingness to improve your circumstances draws dividends. It propels you towards a journey of promise and progression. It helps you advance life into new areas as it flings opens the door to a new chapter. It brings a prosperous time for working with your talents and growing your abilities. Refining your gifts shapes the path ahead into a journey worth growing. Your discipline and dedication draw growth into your career path.

30 Thursday

Exciting opportunities emerge and bring a fantastic time that kickstarts growth and progress in your social life. A positive influence raises confidence and enables you to enjoy rising prospects. You thrive in a more social environment. It offers a clear path forward that draws opportunities and adventure into your life. It plants the seeds for a more connected environment that adds growth and progress to your life. Connecting with kindred spirits brings a welcome boost.

December

Sun	Mon	Tue	Wed	Thu	Fri	Sat
					1	2
3	4	5	6	7	8	9
10	11	12	13	14	15	16
17	18	19	20	21	22	23
24	25	26	27	28	29	30
31						

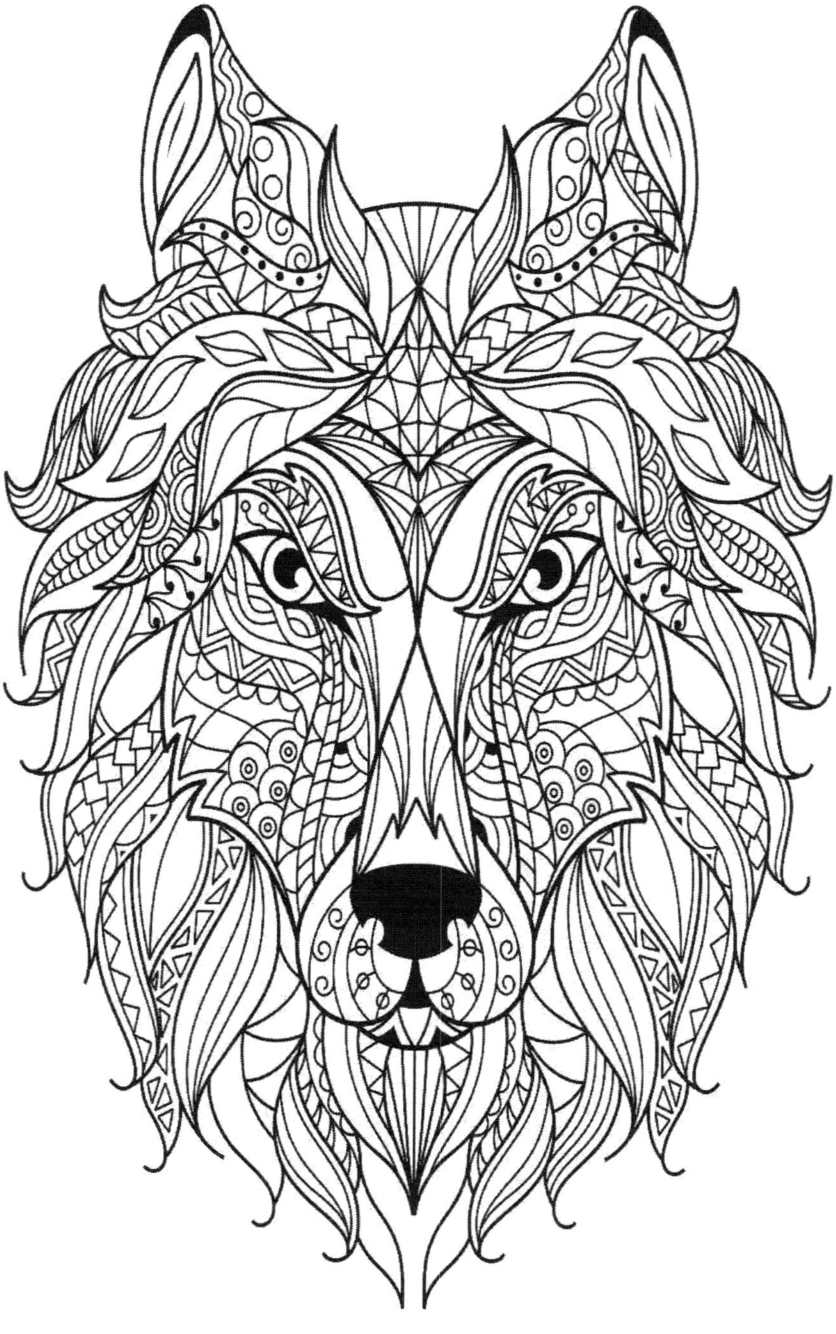

New Moon

Cold Moon

December

1 Friday ~ Mercury ingress Capricorn 14:29

You have a lot of raw energy around your life that seeks expression in tangible forms. Working with your creativity harnesses the essence of innovation to create a unique path forward. Nurturing your capabilities attracts a landmark time that offers remarkable growth and progression. It opens a trailblazing journey towards developing new goals. It connects you with others who forge a community around a common interest.

2 Saturday ~ Mercury sextile Saturn 15:25

Today's Mercury sextile Saturn transit is favorable for organizing and streamlining your workload to create a stimulating and productive environment. Expressing authority and leadership skills create a purposeful and productive environment. It marks a significant chapter that becomes the gateway to growing your life. You get wind of some curious information that unlocks an enriching journey that orients you towards rising prospects.

3 Sunday ~ Venus square Pluto 13:29

Today's aspect could see a flare-up of jealousy or possessiveness. Your romantic partner may feel threatened by heightened social activities and invitations pre-run up to Christmas. Take time to support and boost confidence to help offset the Venus square Pluto aspect. Being aware of these fears' dynamics helps keep relationships healthy and balanced. In the run-up to Christmas, giving extra support to your partner will help keep personal ties connected and stable.

December

4 Monday ~ Mercury at Greatest Elongation 21.3 E, Venus ingress Scorpio 18:48

Change is in the air; news that sees life take an exciting turn is coming. It brings surprise communication and a chance to mingle with friends. It does offer a fruitful time of expansion that ignites inspiration. It turns up the possibilities as you share with friends and get involved with developing group projects. It helps you forge a unique path forward that offers a wellspring of happiness.

5 Tuesday ~ Last Quarter Moon in Virgo 05:50, Venus trine Saturn 22:51

Today's Venus trine Saturn transit is ideal for developing relationships. Self-expression, warmth, and affection flow freely under this favorable aspect. Staying open to fresh ideas and new possibilities brings an active and lively environment. It kicks off sunshine and sparkle in your social life. It offers a suitable landscape to expand your circle of friends. It brings lively discussions and sharing of thoughts and ideas.

6 Wednesday ~ Neptune turns direct in Pisces, 12:38

With Neptune turning direct in Pisces, an extra emotional element adds flavor to your dreams, creativity, and vision. Wistful thinking, goals, and fantasies let you move beyond the material world and escape into fanciful thoughts about future possibilities. It is currently an ideal time for setting intentions and planning goals. Directing your energy towards developing dreams offers new options that cultivate rising prospects.

7 Thursday ~ Hanukkah (begins at sunset)

Your willingness to stay open to new possibilities draws a pleasing result. It brings a shift forward that grows your world in a unique direction. You discover an option that feels like a good fit for your life. Entering a refreshing time, you stay in sync with your vision for future growth. It brings a busy time of developing personal goals as you enjoy a whirlwind of activity in your social life.

December

8 Friday ~ Mercury trine Jupiter 4:04

Mercury's trine Jupiter transit today ignites the possibility of heightened intuition and attracts a chance to chill with friends. Your life shifts and becomes lighter as it gently weaves new prospects into your social life. It syncs you with others who spark insightful conversations that nurture well-being. Harmony and abundance flow into your social life, providing a good sense of connection. Spending time with kindred spirits lays the groundwork for a happy chapter.

9 Saturday

A positive trend is ready to burst forth in your life. As the tides turn in your favor, you enjoy lighter overtones that promote well-being and happiness. Life feels soft and breezy as you engage in a social element that is supportive and nurturing. It begins a time of building stability in foundations that nurture growth in your social world. News and invitations spark an engaging time ahead.

10 Sunday ~ Venus opposed Jupiter 3:34

This astrological transit adds an indulgent vibration and has you wanting to explore hedonism, romance, and magic. The pursuit of pleasure attracts social engagement, relaxation, and unwinding with a leisurely influence restoring well-being in no time. It connects you with people who hold similar values and opinions, bringing a valuable sense of support into your life. Light-hearted social engagement and stimulating conversations nurture fresh ideas that inspire you.

December

11 Monday ~ Mercury sextile Venus 19:22

Communication flows freely into your social life, attracting invitations and mingling opportunities. The Mercury sextile Venus aspect nurtures stable foundations and happiness. Encouraging conversations shared with valued companions helps boost a path that offers well-being and happiness. Sharing with friends brings the right environment to grow friendships. It enables you to find the missing element that holds the key to future happiness.

12 Tuesday ~ New Moon in Sagittarius 23:32

A shift forward connects you with ample time that helps you see life through a new lens of possibility. It brings bonding sessions that hearten and enrich. It connects you with someone with similar interests, and this kindred spirit offers companionship. It brings a time of expansion and adventure that delivers a boost to your world. It draws a social environment that creates a stable foundation from which to grow your life.

13 Wednesday ~ Mercury turns Retrograde in Capricorn 7:08
Geminids Meteor Shower Dec 7-17th

Mercury turns retrograde, seeing communication issues cropping up over the next few weeks. Plans and times quickly become mixed as messages scramble during this more chaotic planetary phase. You may feel unsure about the path ahead but growing your life is the surefire ticket to advancing towards success. Being mindful helps you rise above the drama and embrace enriching your social life. It helps move you towards growth and expansion.

14 Thursday

A strong emphasis on improving circumstances cultivates lighter energy that breaks up the stagnant patterns currently holding you back from achieving your most authentic path. Removing the blocks that stall progress enables you to get busy developing your world in a refreshing direction. It brings a lively atmosphere of social engagement. Life is bustling, active, and dynamic. It fuels inspiration and helps you reclaim vitality under a positive influence.

December

15 Friday ~ Hanukkah (ends at sunset)

Life heads towards an upward trend as it opens a gateway that brings a journey of new adventures. It adds a spontaneous element that attracts clear skies overhead. Invitations crop up that feel like a good fit for your social life. It helps you kick the cobwebs to the curb and enjoy sharing with your broader circle of friends. Networking and mingling promote new ideas and possibilities for future development.

16 Saturday

A gathering you attend with friends lights up growth pathways for your social life. You discover an attentive companion with music and room to circulate at an event. Being open to meeting people and expanding the horizons of your life hits a sweet note for singles this Christmas season. It brings a time of romance, flirting, and magic. A lighter vibration sweeps in to tempt you in a direction that offers promising potential.

17 Sunday

News arrives that kicks off a chapter of improving circumstances. It opens a social environment that connects you with friends, and mingling with people you value attracts rising prospects. It blossoms into a thriving time of sharing thoughtful discussions and entertaining thoughts with others as you grow your world and widen your circle of friends. Investing your time and energy wisely fuels growth in your life.

DECEMBER

18 Monday ~ Mercury trine Jupiter 14:33

Mercury trine Jupiter transit brings optimism, luck, and good news. Information arrives that bodes well for your social life. Indeed, it's easy to make new friends under this favorable influence that sparks social engagement and thoughtful discussions with friendly characters. It helps you tap into opportunities to grow and evolve your life in new directions. You discover a journey that holds promise, which paves the way for a blossoming time to emerge in your life.

19 Tuesday ~ First Quarter Moon in Pisces 18:39

A big reveal opens a refreshing avenue in your social life. It brings lively discussions that fuel creativity and offers inspiration. It puts you in contact with others who provide supportive advice and guidance. Indeed, sharing with friends brings invitations to circulate. As you negotiate a busier environment, you forge deepening friendships that attract happiness and joy. Small changes create an extensive pathway that grows your circle of friends.

20 Wednesday

A touch of magic brings the sparkling energy of positivity into your life this Christmas. Optimism is rife as you release the stress and get involved with sharing with friends and family. New friends enter your life which expands your circle of friends. It offers an active environment that connects you with kindred spirits who share compatible interests and creativity. You trigger a path of developing opportunities by being open to change.

21 Thursday ~ Ursids Meteor Shower Dec 17th – 25th, Venus opposed Uranus 7:04, Mercury sextile Saturn 12:35

Today's Venus opposed Uranus alignment brings growth to personal relationships. Increasing synergy and chemistry could spark a new romance or flirtation opportunity. It brings the gift of companionship as you chart a course towards advancing your circle of friends. You discover room to spread your wings and open up a path that nurtures happiness and well-being.

DECEMBER

22 Friday ~ Sun ingress Capricorn 3:24, Yule/Winter Solstice 03:28, Sun conjunct Mercury 18:53

The Sun conjunct Mercury aspect favors communication. Good news arrives with a flurry of excitement. It provides an important clue about the path ahead as it takes you towards growing your life outwardly. Opportunity comes knocking, creating a pivotal time where you can open up your box of dreams and explore new possibilities. Change and discovery unearth new leads ahead.

23 Saturday ~ Mercury ingress Sagittarius 6:19

Life lightens, bringing laughter, fun, and social engagement to the forefront of your life. It shines the spotlight on sharing with friends as invitations to mingle brings rising prospects into your life. It sets the stage to chase dreams and embrace connectedness as you touch down on a promising journey of developing meaningful bonds in your life. It creates space to nurture new dreams and goals as positive energy flows into your world.

24 Sunday ~ Sun sextile Saturn 17:28

Sun sextile Saturn transit lends patience to family gatherings, which can be a godsend if your family dynamics are challenging. Unleashing some balanced Zen moves can help soothe ruffled feathers. This planetary transit ensures a balanced and stable social gathering that attracts well-being and harmony. A theme of improving circumstances connects with sharing treasured memories. It blossoms into an active and lively environment.

DECEMBER

25 Monday ~ Christmas Day, Venus trine Neptune 17:15

Venus trine Neptune transit is the perfect backdrop to Christmas. It attracts creativity, well-being, and fulfillment. This transit favors singing, music, and delight in the day's celebration and opens the floodgates to a vibrant chapter that nurtures your world. It brings a social aspect that delivers a wellspring of happiness into your life. Spending time with your circle is a source of happiness and joy that harmonizes and restores energy.

26 Tuesday ~ Kwanzaa begins

An influx of potential opens the floodgates to a social environment that expands the borders of your world. It brings invitations that offer social engagement, extending to a time of great inspiration and happiness. It connects you with a tribe of kindred spirits who support your world and provide thoughtful discussions. Immersing yourself in sharing with friends brings companionship and joy to the forefront of your life.

27 Wednesday ~ Cold Full Moon, Moon before Yule in Cancer 0:34, Mercury square Neptune 7:36, Sun trine Jupiter 15:28

The Sun trine Jupiter aspect lights up good fortune across the board. New possibilities blossom as a favorable wind ignites your passion and imagination. Potential moves in leaps and bounds as you connect with a journey that draws inspiration into your life. Creativity heightens, bringing new possibilities to explore. The more you work on improving your circumstances, the easier it is to reinvent and create magic.

28 Thursday ~ Mercury conjunct Mars 0:26, Mars square Neptune 22:15

The Mars square Neptune aspect brings gossip and scandal to your ears. You hear surprising news that feels disconcerting. Suppose something doesn't ring true to your ears. In that case, you should do your own investigating as this transit could draw misinformation leading to confusion. Making your life a priority raises the bar; you can trust your instincts and set barriers around people who cause issues. News ahead cracks the code to a brighter chapter.

December

29 Friday ~ Venus sextile Pluto 6:00, Venus ingress Sagittarius 20:21

The Venus sextile Pluto transit deepens romantic love and grows relationship potential. It brings an expressive time of nurturing a wellspring of abundance. An emphasis on sharing and connecting with friends and companions gives you a positive avenue to channel your excess energy into promoting. It becomes a wise investment as it sparks sunshine and happiness in your life. It brings a lighter time that offers fun, mingling, and social engagement.

30 Saturday

The pace of life settles down to a more manageable hum, bringing more excellent stability into your surroundings. Nurturing balanced foundations creates a solid basis from which to grow your world. Formulating plans and expectations helps craft a vision to head towards next year. It initiates positive growth that draws optimism and happiness into your life. Unique pathways ahead tempt you to develop your talents.

31 Sunday ~ New Year's Eve, Jupiter turns direct in Taurus at 2:41

In a promising sign, Jupiter turns direct on New Year's Eve. It foretells bright blessings, good fortune, and opportunities on the horizon. Unlimited possibilities spark inspiration and wonder in your life. It connects with the flow of abundance and supports a journey of change in your world. New information ahead shines a light on building a bridge toward rising prospects. An area you nurture blossoms into a meaningful path worth growing.

Astrology & Horoscope Books.

Mystic Cat

Manufactured by Amazon.ca
Bolton, ON